MAKING IT COUNT

MAKING IT COUNT

LIFE ISN'T LIVED ON A SPREADSHEET

RYAN POTERACK

LIONCREST
PUBLISHING

MAKING IT COUNT
Life Isn't Lived on a Spreadsheet

ISBN   978-1-61961-714-8 *Paperback*
        978-1-61961-715-5 *Ebook*

DISCLAIMER

Ryan Poterack is an investment advisor offering advisory services through Capital Asset Advisory Services, LLC (CAAS), a registered investment advisor as of the publication of this book.

The opinions expressed in this material represent those of Ryan Poterack and not of CAAS or any registered investment advisor firm.

Nothing contained herein is to be considered a solicitation, research material, an investment recommendation or advice of any kind. Any investments or strategies referenced herein do not take into account the investment objectives, financial situation or particular needs of any specific person. Product suitability must be independently determined for each individual investor.

Some of the investment products discussed herein are considered complex investment products. Such products contain unique risks, terms, conditions and fees specific to each offering. Depending upon the particular product, risks include, but are not limited to, issuer credit risk, liquidity risk, market risk, the performance of an underlying derivative financial instrument, formula or strategy. Return of principal is not guaranteed above FDIC insurance limits and is subject to the creditworthiness of the issuer. You should not purchase an investment product or make an investment recommendation to a customer until you have read the specific offering documentation and understand the specific investment terms and risks of such investment.

CONTENTS

INTRODUCTION 9

1. DON'T LET WEEDS GROW IN YOUR LIFE'S GARDEN! 19

2. STOP "SHOULDING" ON YOURSELF 27

3. SET YOUR EGO ASIDE 39

4. CHECK YOUR BIASES AT THE DOOR 47

5. A DECISION-MAKING PROCESS FOR LIFE 57

6. LET'S MAKE A DEAL WITH THE IRS: 401(K)S, IRAS, AND OTHER "QUALIFIED" ACCOUNTS 67

7. LIFE INSURANCE: A VERY POWERFUL TOOL DESPITE MAXIMUM BIAS 87

8. LONG-TERM CARE INSURANCE: A BAD VISUAL AND BIAS 97

9. ANNUITIES: DON'T BE OLD, SANE, AND BROKE! 105

10. BUY OR RENT, IT'S THE SAME HOUSE 117

11. COLLEGE: CAREER BOON OR BOONDOGGLE? 127

12. ALL DEBT IS NOT CREATED EQUAL 137

13. TILL DEATH DO US PART? 145

14. THE GODFATHER AND DECISION MAKING IN TIMES OF INTENSITY 155

15. DON'T BE AN EASY MARK WHEN YOU INVEST 163

16. IN LIFE, YOU GET WHAT YOU PAY FOR 171

17. NO ONE GETS OUT ALIVE 185

18. YOU DON'T HAVE TO GO IT ALONE 191

ABOUT THE AUTHOR 201

INTRODUCTION

Before you dive in, you may find it helpful to watch and listen to some short, informal, and high-level videos about the various topics we will be covering within this book. Visit poterack.net/investor-resources/videos/ to view any videos that pique your interest.

You may have many goals in life, but having a lot of money is not one of them. Does that surprise you? It may, but it's true.

Rather, your goal is to be able to do what you would do *if* you had a lot of money.

You've been taught that money is great in and of itself. But money is just a means to an end. It's just ink on paper.

Until you exchange money for something you want, it has no inherent value.

Money is freedom. Freedom provides choices!

Have you ever thought, "I wish I'd win the lottery"? If so, you immediately followed that with a thought about what you would do with the money. Because it really isn't about the money. It's about the ability to do what you would do if you had that much money.

You might say, "I wish I'd win the lottery, because I'd quit the job I hate." Or, "My mom could retire." Or, "I'd be able to do a lot of volunteer work without worrying about an income." Your choices would likely be different than those of others who won the same hypothetical lottery.

Winning the lottery is just an event. It certainly would be an exciting event, but the important point is that your life would change because you would have many more choices. The purpose for your money is to provide outcomes that you personally value.

So much of what you have learned about money to this point—even from professionals in the financial services industry—has been about your numbers (quantitative). I refer to your numbers as your "hard facts." Financial professionals may use a boilerplate toolbox and a methodology that treats everyone with the same numbers (age, wealth, income, etc.) in the same way. Are you the same as everyone else? Might your values, attitudes, or circumstances be unique?

If I want to know what you care about—your values, your objectives, your fears, your life experiences, your biases—then who else in the world can give me those answers better than you? Of course, no one can! I refer to this critical information as your "soft facts," which are qualitative. No two people have the exact same soft facts. Therefore, any financial professional who ignores or minimizes the importance of "your story" may not be able to help you achieve your ideal outcomes or hit your goals.

There's no way that anybody, amateur or professional, can predict which stock is going to do better than another stock in the next six months. Even with all the numbers and resources we have as professionals, we cannot predict the future!

In the end, two people with different hard facts and soft facts may use similar products and strategies. Products and strategies are tools. Does a screwdriver drive a screw, help assemble toys, or make a good pointer in a presentation? The answer to all of these is yes.

On occasion, two different objectives may be solved with the same tool. In financial planning, you may buy the same product or choose the same strategy as someone who has very different values and goals. But if you arrive at your decision through a process of critical thinking—deliberate, thoughtful discernment—you're going to feel and be more confident and empowered. That's what this book is about: taking control and *making it count!*

This book is about *making life decisions*, because almost every decision you make involves some financial planning aspect. It's about empowering you to make the decisions that are right for you. It's about giving you the courage to pursue your goals and dreams.

That's no small task. I've been in the financial planning industry for more than half of my life, and during my career, I've seen people whose dreams and hopes kept getting filed down by life and the people around them. Their goals became unrecognizable or forgotten. They were too busy thinking, "I should do this; I should do that." Where did that person's dreams go? What did they want to do when they were fifteen? How did they end up on somebody else's "life assembly line"? How might they, *or you*, get off the "wrong" assembly line?

FINANCIAL PLANNING 101

To illustrate what I mean, let's consider "Financial Planning 101."

Financial Planning 101 typically begins sometime in your twenties or thirties. You're working, and for three or four decades, you try to save what you can. Somewhere along the line, you've been taught your objective is to build a big pile of money. In your sixties—maybe a little younger than that if you've planned well—you retire after building up this big pile of money.

But you don't spend the pile of money! You've been taught to spend only the interest and the dividends from your pile of money—what I call the "scraps"—and to protect the pile itself, which is called your principal. However, I have a very important question for you to ask yourself. If you spend three or four decades building up a pile of money but only spend the scraps, then who gets to spend the pile of money?

You may fear that once you start accessing the principal, once you start nipping at your pile, you could run out of money. I get it! Nobody wants to be old, sane, and broke. That is a bad combination! You may be able to handle two of those three, but the prospect of all three is why people tend to hold on to their principal till they die. Many studies have concluded two key facts to use in your planning. Number one, you will not live on this earth forever. Number two, you can't take your money with you!

Your money in retirement has only two purposes. The first purpose is for *your* fun and lifestyle. The second purpose is for *somebody else's* fun and lifestyle. If you don't spend your money on your own fun and lifestyle, somebody else or some organization will inherit it and spend your money the way they see fit. This is a simple, binary choice. Either you spend it, or someone else does.

If I asked you to tell me what's more important, your fun and lifestyle or passing money to your kids or an organization, probably more than 90 percent of you would say it's your fun and lifestyle. Yet, the clear majority of you may be employing strategies that favor passing on your pile of money to your kids, the Internal Revenue Service (IRS), or various organizations, rather than being able to use it to support your fun and lifestyle.

You may be living below your means while employing strategies to grow your money (which are, of course, appropriate when you are young), rather than strategies to support the lifestyle you want in retirement. You get to make the choice. If it's your goal to provide an inheritance, then by all means do it.

However, you should align your strategies with the outcomes you personally want. Chasing higher market returns is not a strategy. Financial planning is about strategic thinking and efficiency, not simply increasing rate of return. I recognize this may be counterintuitive or unfamiliar to you, but let's move on for now.

PERMISSION TO BE HAPPY

Whether you are twenty or sixty-plus, this book is for you. It's not a get-rich-quick or get-rich-slowly book. It's not a financial textbook, because *your life isn't lived on a spreadsheet.*

This book is about giving you permission not to feel guilty for aspiring to this or for wanting that. It's about finding the people who will support you and about weeding out those who won't. It's about challenging the "shoulds" in your life, confronting your ego and your biases, and learning that it's okay to ask questions. If a doctor says you have a life-threatening disease, you are going to ask questions because this is your life. If a financial advisor says you should use a particular product or strategy, you can expect to receive clear answers to your questions, because this is your life, and you get to *make it count*!

Everyone gets to define what life success is, but you can't

achieve life success without making money decisions. Whether these decisions are big or small, you truly can't avoid money decisions and achieve your life success.

People say money doesn't buy happiness. On the contrary, it may buy a lot of happiness. If it would make you happy to spend more time with your kids, and then you win the lottery, the amount of time you spend with your kids would likely increase. The first thing you need to do is determine what happiness looks like for you—how you define success and what your desired outcomes are. Simply amassing a large amount of money will not make you happy until you exchange your money for that which you enjoy.

That's what this book is designed to do. I'll provide you with a process for critical thinking to guide your decision-making, not only around the products and strategies discussed in this book, but around all of life's big decisions.

I'll share stories from my life and my more than twenty-five years as a financial advisor. I've been very blessed by my successes and very blessed by my failures. My failures, more than my successes, have taught me phenomenal lessons about how to be a better person, father, husband, entrepreneur, and, yes, financial advisor.

From my viewpoint, it's important to work with a trusted advisor who believes your values, goals, and dreams are as important—if not more important—as what's in your bank account.

My goal is to empower you to protect your garden, preserve your dreams, and put you on the path to success—however *you* define it.

Let's get started.

DON'T LET WEEDS GROW IN YOUR LIFE'S GARDEN!

If you've ever tended to a flower or vegetable garden, you know weeds must be managed, or they will choke, limit, or destroy your garden.

Responsible people hang out with responsible people. It's just much easier to be financially successful if you are happy and surrounded by people who uplift you. You have people in your life who make you a better person—a better husband or wife, a better mother or father, a better friend. These people are the flowers in your garden!

And you have people who take away from that: people who drain your time and energy; people who choke off your ambition, your dreams, and your productivity. These are the people who keep putting you down. They throw a wet blanket on your goals and dreams. Typically, they are more comfortable if you don't succeed, because if you improve your economic situation, you may change the basis of your relationship—and that scares them. These people are the weeds in your garden.

We all have people like that in our lives. They may be subtle or passive-aggressive, but they are lethal to your success. Since it's true that misery loves company, if you don't manage those weeds, you will struggle to achieve everything you are capable of achieving.

IDENTIFY THE WEEDS, SO YOU CAN PULL THEM OUT!

Try this exercise:

Take a sheet of paper and draw a line down the middle. On the right side of the line, list the names of the people who lift you up, the people who support you. This doesn't have anything to do with money. The people on the right side of the line are people whose attitude toward life and whose interests align with yours. Keep it simple! Do you feel better, stronger, and more optimistic when you are around the people on the right side of your line?

On the left side of the line, write the names of the people who tear you down, the people who want to pull you back. These people may act nice to your face but undercut you to others. Do you feel better or worse after a conversation with these people?

I'm reminded of a story about collecting crabs that goes something like this. You catch the first crab and put it in your bucket. If you don't watch closely, this crab may get a claw over the edge of the bucket and pull itself out to escape! However, after catching your second crab, you no longer have to worry, because if the first crab attempts to escape, the second crab will pull it back into the bucket (and both will wind up on someone's dinner table!). In this way, the people on the left side of your paper can also be called "crabs" if you wish. I prefer "weeds."

Nobody needs to see this list, so be brutally honest. It takes courage to cut people out of your life, even when you know you'll be better for it.

Sometimes these people are family, or they might be a best friend from thirty years ago in high school. Circle the names that may be difficult to eliminate. For instance, say you identify John as a weed in your garden. You don't feel that you're at your best when John is around. But you might determine that it's important that John remains in your life at this time. Maybe he's your boss. You may have kids and a mortgage, so even though John is a weed and you'd love to snip him out of your garden, you determine it's important that he remains in your life right now. But at least you are thoughtfully and critically assessing that relationship and recognizing there is a price to pay for having John in your life.

Going through an exercise like this, whether or not you put it on paper, helps you evaluate what people bring to your relationships and what they take away.

TRUST IS EVERYTHING

You naturally tend to gravitate toward people who uplift you. Likewise, you know who tears you down, but you may struggle walking away from those people. Typically, they are people you cannot trust. In business and in life, for you to do what you need to do, you often must trust that somebody else will do what they say they're going to do.

For example, Frank was a weed I had to cut out of my life. He was a bighearted, nice guy when we ran into each other. I'd invite him to this or that, and he would always say, "Yeah, I'll come over," or, "Yeah, I'll give you a call," and then he never did. At some point I realized, "Okay, I can have a friendly conversation with Frank, but I don't believe a word he says." Trust is built when you do what you say you're going to do. It's about finishing and not quitting. Quitting can become a habit, and so can finishing. Be a finisher!

You may not control every aspect of finishing, but there is always a moment in your mind when you realize, "I'm not going to be able to get this job done within the time commitment I made." If you committed to me that you'd finish a project by Tuesday at 4:00 p.m., I'm going to appreciate being told at 5:00 p.m. on Monday, not at 3:59 p.m. on Tuesday, that you cannot get it done by the deadline. Everyone appreciates truthfulness. Eventually the truth will be self-evident anyway, so be proactive. This becomes a habit that leads to success in life!

People recognize the moment they're not going to be able to live up to what they have promised, but they make excuses. The worst excuse is "I didn't have enough time." Everyone has the same amount of time, and you get to choose what you want to do with it. I recognize that time is finite, and we may truly run out of time for many reasons. I want to encourage you to be forthright about your choices. Even if the reason you can't honor your commitment is private, it is more honest to say, "Something personal came up," and to indicate when you can meet your obligation, rather than to make time an excuse. If you are candid and share the truth as soon as you know circumstances have changed, then you will build trust with people in your life.

Some people are in the habit of telling stories, but they're lying. A white lie is still a lie. If you tell stories that you know are untrue, and you allow lying to become a habit, your self-esteem will take a hit. You won't feel good about yourself, or you will be in denial, which is to say that you are being untruthful to yourself! This undermines your happiness and your achievements.

If others let you down often enough, it may undermine your success, too. We all fail and fall well short of perfection. We also have complete control over facing up to and learning from these failures.

"Lie," "truth," and "fail" may seem like harsh words. To me, they are precise and descriptive. Words matter, and you likely don't want to use them to hurt anyone. However, being clear with and about yourself, and with (if not about) everyone around you, builds a habit of not making excuses. Of course, life is rarely black and white, but being completely honest with yourself is a good practice that leads to better decision making and life success!

As a business owner and entrepreneur, if I have somebody who will tell me the truth every single time—even if it's a truth I don't want to hear—I can work with that all day long. That's gold. If people become known for doing what they say they're going to do, and for being forthright and candid, they are the kind of people you want in your garden and in your life because *you can count on them.*

To sum up, being miserable is not good for your economic situation. It's difficult to be your best at whatever creates your money if you're unhappy. If you're doing something that you've always wanted to do—maybe starting a business—then the weeds are the naysayers who will try to pull you back when you step outside the norm. They may "should" on you. Weeds stifle creativity and, potentially, your psychological and economic health.

In the next chapter, we'll look at the dreaded "shoulds" and how you can get off someone else's life assembly line.

STOP "SHOULDING" ON YOURSELF

I can remember the feeling of wanting to be older. My ambition wanted real-life accomplishments!

I wanted to check all the boxes, get my career going, buy a house, get married, have kids, and so on. Now I look back and wonder, "What was I thinking?" I wasn't thinking—not for myself, anyway.

I was "shoulding" on myself. I was on somebody else's life assembly line. I was living a life story other people wanted me to live. I accept 100 percent responsibility for this, but eventually I had to decide whether to "should" or to get off the pot—the life assembly line on which I'd been placed!

A BORN ENTREPRENEUR

If you become an amazing baseball player or a renowned musician, chances are it's because you were born with a certain talent. And people likely recognized this athletic or musical talent when you were young. But for other areas of expertise, such as being an entrepreneur, people seem less able to recognize unique abilities. However, as I look back on my life, two stories in particular tell me that I was born to be in business for myself.

In 1975, I was nine years old. We lived about a mile away from a five-and-dime store that sold all manner of goods, including candy.

At that time, at least where I lived, nobody thought twice about allowing a nine-year-old to ride a bike a mile alone. Of course, there were limitations. I'm the oldest of my siblings, and my two brothers, who were six and four, along with my toddler sister, were too young to go to the store alone.

This may shock you, but as kids we liked candy! I sensed a business opportunity. I would ride to the store and buy candy for a penny, a nickel, and a dime. Then I would return home, set up a candy shop in my room, and sell the candy for a nickel, a dime, and a quarter.

I put forth the effort and took the risk that I might buy

candy my brothers didn't particularly like and wouldn't want to buy from me. Over time, that risk straightened itself out—my first foray into market research, if you will. I provided something of value to my younger brothers, who didn't have access to what they wanted—candy! I was rewarded for my work and investment with money. I look back on that experience today, and I understand that not every nine-year-old would have thought to do what I did.

About six years later, when I was fifteen, I had a newspaper route. I wanted to play baseball and other sports, but the papers were delivered after school, typically around 3:30 p.m. To both play sports and keep my paper route, I hired my brothers, who were then twelve and ten. I hired one brother to deliver the newspapers. I hired the other brother to do the collecting, because you didn't just deliver the papers in those days. You also went around once a month, knocked on the door of every newspaper subscriber on your route—with your two-ring binder and perforated tabs in hand—and collected the money. After paying each brother "employee," I kept a nifty profit.

My brothers were doing the labor; however, I still had the responsibility to ensure that the work was properly completed. It's as true today in my businesses as it was then. If somebody didn't get their newspaper on time, I couldn't say, "Well, that's my brother's fault." I accepted personal responsibility regardless of who tossed the paper on the porch. I either succeeded or failed to have newspapers delivered to subscribers. This was my truth then.

I provided employment to both of my brothers, who couldn't get the paper route on their own. I could go out for athletics and run a business while still in high school. Being a finisher doesn't mean you must do everything, but it does mean you accept personal responsibility for finishing your commitments!

How did I decide to do these things? I think it was as organic as putting a paintbrush and canvas in front of a budding artist and coming back an hour later and saying, "Well, how did they do that?"

I certainly didn't learn to be an entrepreneur from my parents. I was raised in a traditional household. My parents are great, but their path to success was far different from mine. My father had an MBA and was an executive for John Deere. He was a traditional corporate executive, not an entrepreneur. My mom is a great mom—she ran our home very effectively, but chose never to work outside the home.

My parents shaped my worldview, but they did not recognize or acknowledge that I was a born entrepreneur.

Aside from my candy and newspaper examples, I mowed lawns, shoveled snow, "published" a neighborhood newspaper, organized neighborhood ball games, and sold items through Boy Scouts, among many other examples of exceptional initiative. This was not recognized as a unique ability to be encouraged and uniquely supported.

I was and still am introverted. When I was young, I struggled to fit in because I was different. My differences were related to mindset. I remember vividly my ideas and dreams being tamped down by my parents. They didn't want me to be disappointed if I failed to realize my ideas and dreams. However, their approach ensured my feeling of disappointment at a very young age and introduced me to what I now refer to as the "shoulds," which place so many barriers in the way of our personal and professional growth.

The path to success imprinted on me by my parents and the people in my parents' circle—because there tends to be a common value system within circles—included a lot of "shoulds": we should graduate high school; we should go to college; we should get married; we should have kids, and we should find a career in corporate America that should have benefits. "Should" was all over the place!

When you have that kind of traditional upbringing, you're often not given license to be different, weird, or think freely. So, I never fit in. I'm not a follower. Actually, I can follow great and truthful leadership through a fire with a gasoline suit on! But I can no longer follow simply because someone says I should.

I have a huge desire to understand things, and I ask a lot of questions. In the corporate world, you often must follow people and a doctrine that you may not believe in or understand. If you ask questions, the corporate types don't necessarily want to give you the real answers. Truth and candor may seem like scarce resources in many corporations, if not in the world generally.

I've had a great life so far, and I've had some phenomenal success in terms of how it's traditionally interpreted, which is economic. At fifty, I'm just getting warmed up! Most people use money as a measuring stick for success in life—and by that measure, my parents have been very successful—yet my path has been completely different from theirs. Not better or worse, but very different. My parents traveled the path best for them, and I eventually found the best path for me.

I was a born entrepreneur stuck on somebody else's life assembly line, with "should" all over me. That cost me dearly. I was kicked in the teeth by divorce—the biggest failure of my life—which led to financial failures.

Here's my paradox: I'm absolutely certain I could not have achieved as much as I have in my life if I hadn't experienced my failures, including my divorce. This is my truth. I was thirty and had largely lived someone else's story to that point. This life assembly line was moving me along, all comfy-looking on the outside but painfully unhappy on the inside.

While it's unfortunate that it took massive disruption to wake me up, it was a blessing in disguise, because I got off the assembly line. I could have withdrawn or felt sorry for myself, which I did for a short time before I was saved, literally and spiritually. I began taking stock of my garden and pulling weeds.

I left the corporate world to become a business owner—an independent financial advisor—and never looked back. The spirit that led me to start a candy shop in my bedroom was rekindled, and that fire to learn, grow, and help people has led me to owning several businesses.

I mentioned being saved. In 2002, I was born again as a Christian, which continues to be an awesome source of my strength. I could not have achieved as much as I have in my life without meeting the strongest person I've ever known. My wife, Dawn, is brilliant. Dawn pushed me off the corporate assembly line and steeled my vision of leading the life of an entrepreneur as I was meant to live. She is also an outstanding weed-picker! Her strength guided me then and has every day since.

I've known others who have been knocked down and gotten back up, as I did. But what if you didn't have to do that? There is a lot of truth in the statement, "What doesn't kill you makes you stronger." What if, instead of waking up when you're thirty and thinking, "Get this packaging off me," you find an easier way to step off somebody else's life assembly line, with less disruption and heartache? I'm sharing my experiences so that you may have the strength to do so!

ARE YOU ON SOMEBODY ELSE'S LIFE ASSEMBLY LINE?

You can step off somebody else's life assembly line, if it's not serving you well, by questioning the dreaded "shoulds"—you should go to college; you should get married; you should buy a house; you should have a 401(k); you should live off the "scraps" of your retirement savings, and on and on.

For example, people say, "Everybody should go to college." Well, I disagree. It's just like yesterday's high school. If everybody goes to college, then college isn't special. A lot of kids go to college and don't find a job. College degrees were much more special and indicative of financial success for my parents' generation than mine, and young people today are bypassing conventional education to pursue businesses as careers in startling numbers!

There are certain disciplines where you need a degree—if you're going to be an engineer or a scientist, for example. But for many people who get a liberal arts or business degree, which I have, it may be a grotesque waste of money. If college is about learning, there are nearly infinite ways to learn in this digital age, aside from paying a small fortune to a college or university. Working toward a degree is a big part of the assembly line that is damaging a lot of people, given all the college debt. We'll look at this more in chapter 11.

In other words, *life isn't lived on a spreadsheet*. This is your life, and you get to *make it count!*

Here's another example of questioning "shoulds." Let's start with a sixty-five-year-old couple. Statistically speaking, the man is going to live to be eighty-five, the woman eighty-seven. One of the two may very well be alive at ninety-two (50 percent probability). If we think about that period of twenty to twenty-five years, there's typically more bounce in a person's step between sixty-five and seventy-five than between seventy-five and eighty-five.

But often, people are making financial decisions as if they're going to live forever with the same level of energy and good health. Conventional thinking assumes you are going to consume and spend exactly the same throughout the remaining twenty or twenty-five years of your retirement life, and then one day it's over. *That's just not how life works.*

Your reality, based on applying critical thinking, may lead you to do what's on your bucket list when you first retire or during the first ten to fifteen years of retirement. You have a lot of fun, you travel, and then you say, "I don't want to go to Hawaii for the fifth time. I don't want to fight airports. I want a good book, a bottle of wine, and the grandkids over to visit for two hours. That's a great day!" That doesn't cost much. Your reality might mean spending more money early in retirement, and then your discretionary spending may level out or possibly decline later in life.

Yet, I see how people choose to live throughout retirement when strategic financial planning is not used. Let's examine this scenario with a sixty-five-year-old couple and assume they have $1 million saved. This $1 million represents their "pile of money" or "principal." Often, this couple will remain on the assembly line of conventional thinking by not touching their pile of $1 million. They think, "I've got to preserve that million dollars. I don't know how long I'm going to live." Hello? Please. You know you're not going to live forever!

Say, at age seventy-five, this couple doesn't have $1 million in principal; they have $700,000. *That's okay.* It means they had $300,000 more fun than another couple on the assembly line who's still got $1 million and is only living off the "scraps." At eighty-five, if they have "only" $400,000 left, then they had another $300,000 worth of fun, versus the couple who is only enjoying the "scraps" and acting as if they will live forever.

Which eighty-five-year old couple would you rather be? There's no right or wrong answer, but this is a choice! You may choose to have more fun in whatever way you define fun (fishing, charity work, travel, etc.) and, therefore, choose to pass on less inheritance. You may choose to live less of a lifestyle so your heirs may live more of a lifestyle after you die.

The point is that *you get to choose*. Which is more important? Your fun and lifestyle or passing the money on to the kids? It's your choice. If the life assembly line you're on is working for you, that's great. If it's not, *you get to step off*. You don't have to make yourself live beneath your means, or not do something you can afford to do, because of the dreaded "shoulds."

You may feel overwhelmed with all you "should" be doing. It's okay to *slow down to speed up*. Life is a marathon, not a sprint. By "slow down," I mean take stock of where you are versus where you want to be in life. Apply critical thinking. Be truthful to yourself, and if you are blessed to have a partner like my wife, Dawn, is to me, then by all means share your truth.

Candidly, you may benefit from cutting a lot of things or behaviors out of your life. It's okay to do so. It's not going to be a tragedy. But first, you have to get out of your own way. You have to let go of your ego and check your biases at the door. This may be difficult, and we'll examine how to do this in the next two chapters.

SET YOUR EGO ASIDE

When your ego drives your decisions, you act against your own self-interest, and you may not even know it.

Think about what you say when someone asks you, "Hey, how are things going?" Probably 99 percent of the time you're going to say, "Everything is great." Well, maybe this is true, and maybe this is not true. You could be responding without thinking, because most of the time you're concerned about what other people think. You are going along to get along. This may seem like a harmless example. I agree. But consider this: bad habits and good habits are reinforced by repetitive behavior. Going along to get along can be the first step onto someone else's life assembly line and may be harmful to your financial health.

YOUR EGO CAN LEAD YOU ASTRAY

When you are going along to get along, you may be spending money you don't have on things you don't want or need. Your ego may compel you to "keep up with the Joneses."

For example, you might decide that you want to buy a six-thousand-square-foot house. You don't need or even want that large of a house, but you want to be in the neighborhood with other people you look up to, people for whom having that size and type of house is a mark of success. Or you might buy a particular car because you want to be seen as the type of person who drives that kind of car.

These are significant financial decisions affecting your wealth, cash flow, and financial security, but they may be done entirely out of ego. There's nothing wrong with buying expensive cars, homes, or anything else. I'm challenging you to be self-aware about *why you are making those decisions.* I absolutely do not want to "should" on you by saying you shouldn't buy expensive cars or whatever you like!

Think of it this way. Suppose you and I were on a secluded island, and I asked you, "How much does it really matter that you got that $85,000 Mercedes?" How would you respond? If you and I were the only two people on the planet, would it matter to you? Are you better served having that car, or would you rather spend the money on something else, such as weekly massages? There is no right or wrong answer; *there is only your answer*. Maybe you have always wanted a Mercedes! If you bought the Mercedes because of how the people in your garden would view you driving a Mercedes, then is that worth the price? It may or may not be.

Throughout this book, I am not providing you with answers you *should* follow. I am encouraging you to ask yourself more and better questions.

Another area in which ego can come into play is around your children. As a parent, talking with friends, the conversation may turn to what your children are doing after high school. You might want to be able to say, "My son's going to Wharton," or, "My daughter's going to Stanford." We all want to be proud of our children *and* have a good story to tell those people in our garden.

Much of this is ego. Maybe other parents in your garden or social circles have children enrolled in what are thought of as prestigious—and expensive—colleges and universities. Your twenty-two-year-old daughter may be on her own assembly line—not yours—by going to community college, teaching gymnastics to young children, and being happy in her own choices. Too often, parents put so much pressure on their kids. They are well intentioned, but their egos tell them they need a great story to tell their friends and colleagues.

Ultimately, there are no right or wrong choices. This is not about denigrating somebody else's choices; it's about not making choices for somebody else's reasons.

This situation is not too far removed from the weeds in the garden we discussed earlier. The truth is the truth is the truth, but you may feel that you want a story to tell some of the people in your life. If you feel you can't proudly tell someone the truth, then that person might be a weed! You may not be able to remove them from your garden, but you can minimize the time you spend with them and the influence they have on your decisions.

NO ONE WANTS TO APPEAR STUPID

Sometimes people let their egos get in the way of admitting what they don't know. I see this all the time in my financial planning practice. People nod their heads because they don't want to admit they have questions. They don't want to appear stupid to others or to themselves. There truly are no stupid questions, only people who are stupidly threatened by questions.

Think about ordering wine on a first date. Unless you're a

connoisseur, it's likely you might be a little nervous about ordering wine. This can be pretty scary when you just want to have a good bottle of wine and enjoy a meal with great company. While that's the outcome you want, you've got to order from an intimidating wine menu, and you may hesitate to ask for help. That's your ego taking over.

The same thing is true for technology. There are new tools, toys, and apps coming out all the time. Nobody likes to feel stupid, and technology can make you feel that way. But here's the thing: your insecurity gets in the way of making good decisions. Asking questions when you don't understand something or are in unfamiliar situations does feel uncomfortable. However, as you build this habit, the discomfort goes away, and you also learn much more!

It's true that there is a lot of information out there about financial products and services. You can do a quick Google search for almost anything you want to know. *But information isn't knowledge, and knowledge certainly isn't wisdom.*

You don't need to know all the details of how various financial products work, any more than I need to understand the chemistry underlying the prescription the doctor gives me. I do want to understand why he prescribed this course of treatment rather than another, and if I have questions or concerns about whether it's the right treatment for me, it's up to me to ask! The doctor is the expert in medicine, but I'm the expert on me. In medicine, this concept is often referred to as *shared decision making.*

In much the same way, there is no need for you to feel inadequate or insecure in discussions with a financial advisor, because you—*and only you*—are the expert on what you want your money to do for you. The products and strategies a financial advisor offers are nothing but tools designed to help you reach your desired outcomes.

Ask questions! If you don't understand something, speak up. It's okay to do so. If the advisor doesn't receive your questions well, then seek another advisor.

It's not just you. Ignorance about money is widespread. Little to nothing is done in high school or college to help people understand even everyday financial decisions, such as taking out a mortgage, balancing a checkbook, or whether it's better to lease or buy a car.

I know financial decision making may seem scary, but don't let your ego or your insecurity stop you from getting all the information you need to make decisions that are right for you. Remember, there are no right or wrong answers or good or bad choices. *There are only the choices that are best for you.*

Sometimes it's not what you don't know, but what you think you do know, that can stand in the way of making good financial decisions. We'll examine biases in the next chapter.

CHECK YOUR BIASES
AT THE DOOR

Bias is fiction, pure and simple, but this is less obvious than it may seem.

You make better decisions with facts and truthful information, and no one wants to believe they have any biases. You may assume others have them, especially if they are trying to sell you something. But everyone has acquired various biases—conscious or unconscious—that stand in the way of making good decisions about money and life. The more you understand this, the more you can be aware of and challenge these biases, resulting in decisions that are best for you.

In my business, I frequently encounter unconscious biases about specific financial products or strategies. However, there is no such thing as a positive or negative product or strategy; these are just different tools you may use to help achieve your desired outcomes.

No one is born with positive or negative feelings about stocks or bonds, life insurance or annuities, and so on. Your experiences have created your biases. Step one is to accept the fact that a bias is based on your personal experience, which is unique to you. Step two is to separate what is real from what is hearsay. With financial products and strategies, you want to understand what they do and what they don't do. Negative past experiences, yours or others', almost always come from lack of knowledge about the chosen product or strategy prior to implementation.

The negative experience likely had nothing to do with the product or strategy and everything to do with using the wrong tool for your desired outcome at the time. You might have made the wrong choice out of ignorance, or because you were dealing with an unscrupulous financial professional, or because you assumed that what was good for a friend must be good for you without regard for your unique "soft facts." Nobody wants to repeat mistakes, so you may blame the product or strategy instead of accepting personal responsibility for your choices. As a result, you narrow your thinking and limit your choices going forward.

PAST EXPERIENCES DON'T PREDICT FUTURE OUTCOMES

There is a saying in my industry that conveys the fact that none of us has a crystal ball when it comes to the financial markets: "Past performance is not indicative of future results." In much the same way, the fact that you had a bad experience with a product or service doesn't mean the product or service was bad. It may simply mean that it wasn't the product or service for the situation you faced.

When you're young, all your friends are getting started on their careers. Maybe you had a friend who got into the real estate business or a friend who started selling life insurance. You were a prospect for them, primarily because of the relationship you had. This was helpful to them, and it may or may not have been helpful to you. You might have purchased something on the strength of the trust you had in this relationship, even though you didn't know that much about the product or strategy. Maybe it turned out that it wasn't a good fit for you.

Or you might have chosen a product or strategy because your neighbor, your uncle, or your brother thought it was a good idea. You respect them, so you figured what they chose must be good for you. That would be like if you hurt your own shoulder but took the medication my doctor gave me for my shoulder injury. You may be dealing with a unique problem that requires a different solution.

Likewise, your financial situation and your desired outcomes may be vastly different from those of the individuals in your garden. There is no one-size-fits-all choice in financial planning or in life.

These experiences color your views. You think, "Oh, I got into this, and I got ripped off. I won't be fooled again." You are deciding based on bias, not on fact. This may be very costly to you!

REVEAL YOUR BIASES, SO YOU CAN ROOT THEM OUT

To unpack these unconscious biases, try an exercise that I use with my clients. In the following table, I've listed eleven common financial products.

Check the box that corresponds to how you feel about each one. Each product will give you a positive feeling, a negative feeling, or a neutral feeling. If you're unfamiliar with the product, put a question mark in the neutral category. Don't spend more than a few minutes on this exercise; just make note of your initial gut reaction.

PRODUCT	POSITIVE	NEUTRAL	NEGATIVE
Stocks			
Mutual Funds			
Variable Annuities			
Exchange Traded Funds			
REITs			
Government Bonds			
Corporate Bonds			
Fixed Annuities			
CDs			
Long-Term Care Insurance			
Life Insurance			

When you are done with the exercise, if you have any "positive" or "negative" checkmarks, then ask yourself, "Where does that positive bias or negative bias come from?" Say, for example, you have a negative impression of buying individual stocks. Maybe it's because your parents invested in individual stocks and lost money. Write that down. That fact is personal and important to you, but it has nothing to do with the benefits or drawbacks of owning individual stocks. Perhaps your parents were given bad advice. Maybe they tried investing on their own and didn't know enough about what they were doing.

If you still have doubts, ask yourself whether you would accept this reasoning from another person making a case against buying individual stocks or any other product. You will quickly see that bias isn't objective reasoning; it is based on historical experience, but it is not a current truth.

If your answer is "neutral," then you can move forward by asking, "What does the product actually do, and what doesn't the product do?" Now you are objectively pursuing what is in your best interest.

Throughout this exercise, you will think of other people's biases and opinions. Some of these people may be the weeds you need to get out of your garden. Put product benefits and limitations in writing. Whenever you start having positive or negative feelings, put them in writing, too. It's often easier to examine what you're thinking when it's right in front of you in black and white. I'm sure you will also have plenty of questions, because you don't know what you don't know. This exercise may prepare you for a phenomenal and informative discussion with a financial professional. I've found this conversation to be as important as any when building a plan that's in the best interest of the client!

KEEP AN OPEN MIND

Here's how I use this exercise with clients. After completing the exercise and listening to the origin of the client's biases, I explain the following.

If you have a bias against a product that isn't appropriate for your situation, we won't waste any time on it. We can move forward without this particular bias negatively impacting you.

Bias works against your self-interests, though, when you have negative biases about products or strategies that are objectively in your best interest. Negative bias closes your mind to possibilities that are worth understanding. That's why working with a fiduciary is so important.

Fiduciaries have a professional responsibility to not go along with a client's bias simply to make a sale. A fiduciary must confront bias for what it is. As a fiduciary myself, I have a responsibility to explain why certain products or strategies are in my clients' best interest based on their desired outcomes. Making decisions for reasons of bias—the client's or the advisor's—is contrary to the fiduciary standard. (See chapter 16 for a further discussion of what it means to act as a fiduciary.)

Often, I will say, "I think this strategy might help you. Let's do our due diligence." Typically, when confronted by their own bias, most clients want to learn more.

Of course, I never forget whose money it is. If a client says, "No, I don't want that option on the table," then we may move on. However, if I believe a product or strategy can help them achieve their desired outcomes, I won't avoid what may be a difficult conversation.

In other words, I must be as concerned with what I call the "soft facts" as I am with the hard facts. I know my client's assets and how much income they have. But that knowledge tells me nothing about what their motivations are, what their biases are, what their life experiences have been, and what they want to do with the rest of their life. Much of my work is quantitative, but I pay as much, if not more, attention to the qualitative. You should expect no less from any advisor with whom you work. Remember, *you are the expert on you*. Your expertise in this area matters!

Ultimately, my objective—and the objective of any advisor, whether in financial services, law, or medicine—is to do what's best for you *as you define it*. Fiduciaries are in the business of building consultative relationships. However, I may only do what is in your best interest that you allow me to do. Often, I see otherwise rational, intelligent people make decisions not in their own best interest for reasons disconnected from facts. This is most often the result of not getting past their own biases. It is my responsibility to assist clients in navigating their biases, which is more of a challenge than you may think.

I'm also in the business of helping clients make better decisions, not only about financial products and strategies, but about life. In the next chapter, I'll introduce a process for critical thinking. You may use it to step over the weeds, set your ego aside, and challenge your biases on the way to making great decisions that are best for you!

5

A DECISION-MAKING PROCESS FOR LIFE

Money is such a common thing that it's difficult to admit when you don't know much about it.

Money is in everyone's pockets. You use it to buy things all the time, because money is a medium of exchange. But you don't necessarily learn how to make financial decisions that are in your own best interest. This is likely because you are not applying critical thinking to your decision-making.

STRENGTHEN YOUR CRITICAL-THINKING MUSCLE

Critical thinking is like a muscle: the more you use it,

the stronger it gets. For some, critical thinking comes naturally; for others, it requires more work.

The following is a process I use to arrive at decisions that are best for me. It's a set of three questions, which, at this point, I run through quickly and often subconsciously. Over time, this process may become second nature for you, too. You can use it not only for making financial decisions but also to make any decision, large or small. I'll outline the questions here and explain them in more detail below.

- What outcome am I seeking?
- What are my deal breakers?
- Why wouldn't I want to do this?

SEPARATE WANTS FROM NEEDS

The first question, "What outcome am I seeking?" can also be asked as, "What do I want?" And wants are different from needs. Assuming your basic needs are met, when was the last time you said, "I want to breathe," or, "I want shelter," or, "I want clothes"? These are examples of needs, not wants.

Why is this difference important? You may be struggling to tell yourself, and others, what you want. You often feel you must justify your wants to other people, whereas you never feel that you must justify your needs.

Remember, *this is about you*. If you have someone in your life to whom you must justify your wants, ask yourself if that person is a weed. Anyone who uplifts you would want you to get everything you want!

When you distinguish between wants and needs, you are developing a habit of truth telling. And that habit strengthens your decision-making ability. You increase the speed with which you make confident decisions, because you eliminate time wasted lying to yourself. With objectivity and enhanced confidence, you improve the quality of your decision-making.

NO SMILE, NO DEAL!

Everything in life has benefits and limitations. Some limitations may be overcome by the corresponding benefits, but some limitations are deal breakers. What are *your* deal breakers in seeking the outcomes you want?

You may not think of something as a deal breaker until you are faced with it. Therefore, with every potential deal breaker—which can be defined as an issue that's without clear benefits or that's against your values—ask yourself,

"Am I willing to accept this with a smile?" If you cannot, then it is a deal breaker.

Write down these deal breakers. Be decisive. If something doesn't make you smile instantly, if it doesn't give you a good feeling right away, then it may be a deal breaker. Put it in the deal breaker category for now. No smile, no deal! You are negotiating with yourself at this point, so be honest in identifying what you are willing and not willing to do to achieve your outcomes.

Getting your desired outcome while setting aside all possible deal breakers would be ideal. You will also have greater clarity and spend less time debating with yourself if you "park" the deal breakers to the side and keep your thoughts rolling.

Depending on the decision you are trying to make, identifying deal breakers can be an emotional challenge. If necessary, set your list aside and come back to it in a calmer moment.

If you cannot reach your desired outcome, your thirst for that outcome will likely increase. With increased desire (people naturally want what they cannot have), you may conclude that some of the items on your list are only "borderline deal breakers," which you might reconsider by taking into account the enhanced perceived benefits of your desired outcome.

For example, say you want to lose ten to fifteen pounds, and you decide exercise will help. You are trying to figure out the best time to fit exercise into your schedule. You take out a piece of paper and write down your deal breakers. They look something like this:

> I'm not a morning person, so exercising in the morning is a deal breaker. I work from 9:00 a.m. to 5:00 p.m., so exercising during the day is a deal breaker. I must cook dinner and take care of the kids, and I must be in bed by 9:00 p.m., so exercising in the evening is a deal breaker.

Now look at your list. If there is no way to get to your desired outcome based on these multiple deal breakers, step back and reassess the situation. Compare your weakest deal breaker with your motivation to truly get the outcome you want. Perhaps you'll then decide you can get up half an hour earlier and go to the gym before work. Or you'll ask your spouse to cook dinner while you use the treadmill in the den.

On the other hand, if you decide that even your weakest deal breaker is still a deal breaker, maybe you will be more at peace with what you weigh. Perhaps you've been thinking you "should" lose the weight, because of how others might view you, but now you've made the decision that's right for you.

You can apply this process to all decisions, including financial ones. If you have a negative bias about a specific financial product or strategy, is it truly a deal breaker? Or is your ego getting in the way? Are you biased against it because of a previous negative experience, or is it truly something you just don't want to consider, for whatever reason?

Sadly, some people carry a few deal breakers around with them. I met a teacher in her mid-thirties who told me she had only fourteen more years to work until she qualified for a pension. I thought that was such a sad thing to say. She's young, and she's considering the next fourteen years of her professional life as something to get through so she can get a pension. That's carrying some serious deal breakers. There may be light at the end of her tunnel, but that is a long tunnel!

You might open your mind and consider, "What's truly important to me?" Would you tell your child, "Son, go find work where you can count down the number of days until you get a pension"? Yet, people find themselves in that situation, and then they feel trapped, but they built the trap themselves. You make choices, so you must be clear about what you want and be truthful about what you are willing, and not willing, to do to meet your objectives.

MAKE THE OPPOSITE CASE

This last step in the decision-making process is counter-intuitive, and because of that, it can be very powerful. Once you've decided what you want and have removed or addressed the deal breakers, stop and ask yourself, "Why wouldn't I want do to this?" Argue the opposite case for the decision you're about to make.

I see this a lot in group settings, where there tends to be a momentum for doing something. Often, that momentum is led by the person who talks most confidently, whether they're right or wrong. They're telling you what's good good good about this product or that service. But you may not be getting the whole story. The Toyota salesman is not talking positively about the Fords.

I do this step with my staff because it's fun and effective. When everybody determines that something we're planning to do is good, I'll turn the tables and ask, "Why wouldn't we want to do this?" Just put a little bit of energy behind making the case against the decision, because there's always a case against it for those who are looking.

Say you've decided to buy a house. You determine that it will help you get what you want—a stable home in a neighborhood that has good schools for your kids. You can remove any deal breakers, deciding, for example, that the extra fifteen minutes it adds to your commute will be worth it. Now ask yourself why you wouldn't want to buy this house. Perhaps the down payment will be a stretch. Maybe there's a chance you'll be transferred to another state before you can build much equity. In the end, if you still decide to buy the house, you'll know that it was the absolute best decision for you. You've gotten what you want, you've dealt successfully with your deal breakers, and the reasons for not doing it were not strong enough to deter you. You've strengthened your critical-thinking muscle, and it's working well for you!

PUT YOUR SHARPENED TOOLS TO USE

This process is designed to keep your thoughts moving forward and avoid getting stuck. The correct decision for you will become self-evident. You will genuinely know the moment you've made the decision that's best for you, and you will feel confident about it.

Equally important, you will develop a decision-making

habit. The stress related to decisions is due to not being confident about them. A decision lacking confidence remains in the present; you continue to wonder if you made the correct decision, and you may be relentlessly tormented. On the other hand, a confident decision is always in the past; you turn the page and move forward! You will make mistakes because we all do, but you will stop vacillating over decisions, which wastes a lot of your precious energy.

Over time, you'll find that you can work through this process quickly. You'll make better decisions with clarity and confidence.

Now you're ready to consider some of the financial products and strategies that may help you achieve your desired outcomes. You've learned to question the "shoulds" that put you on someone else's assembly line, you've checked your ego, you've challenged your biases, and you've applied critical thinking to many of your decisions. Your tools are now sharpened and ready to use!

LET'S MAKE A DEAL WITH THE IRS: 401(K)S, IRAS, AND OTHER "QUALIFIED" ACCOUNTS

When you retire, you don't want money from a retirement account; you just want money to enjoy your lifestyle in retirement.

When you go to the grocery store or book a cruise, they don't ask you where the money came from. It doesn't matter. Likewise, when your son or daughter goes to college, they don't want money that's only from a college savings account. They just want money to pay for room, board, and books.

The key, of course, is that you must be disciplined about saving for retirement, and this is why 401(k)s have become so popular. They make it easier for you to save. The money comes out of your paycheck. You may not even notice it.

People think of 401(k)s and Individual Retirement Accounts (IRAs) as investments. But a 401(k) or an IRA is not an investment. If you use these strategies, you are not making an investment decision—you are making a tax decision. By choosing either a tax-deferred or a tax-free account, you are deciding when you want to pay taxes on your retirement savings. It's that simple.

Remember, there tends to be forward momentum for making one decision over another. You may be going along with so-called conventional wisdom about tax-deferred accounts without examining critically whether it's best for you. That's like when you wanted to attend a party because all your friends were going and your parents asked, "If everyone else was jumping off a bridge, would you do it, too?" You might not want to follow your friends off that bridge or into a traditional 401(k). Let's see why.

MAKE A DEAL WITH THE IRS

When you open a traditional 401(k), a traditional IRA, or a similar tax-deductible, tax-deferred account, you are making a deal with the Internal Revenue Service (IRS) not to pay taxes at today's tax rate, but rather to pay taxes at an unknown tax rate in the future.

Let's say I approach you with the following business deal:

> You and I are going to partner on this deal. You're going to put up all the money and take all the investment risk. I'm not going to put up any of the money or take any of the risk. Then, when you want to harvest profits, I'll let you know how much of the money is yours and how much is mine. I'll tell you when and how much money you can take. Does that sound like a good idea?

You probably would think twice about taking that deal, but that's what you're doing when you invest in these types of accounts. Before 1979, 401(k)s didn't exist, but now they have become a very popular way of accumulating retirement savings. If you're fifty or older, you might even say to your kids who are starting their career, "Boy, I wish I had a 401(k) when I was your age." You might encourage them to save until it hurts. Well, let's apply critical thinking to Jennifer's situation to see whether that makes universal sense.

Jennifer, age thirty-five, works at ABC Corporation and decides that she's going to contribute $10,000 a year to her traditional 401(k), which means that on her federal tax return, her $100,000 income is only $90,000. Her traditional 401(k) contribution is made with pretax dollars. Jennifer has determined, "I don't want that $10,000 income today, at today's tax rate. I want it to sit in this traditional 401(k) and grow over time, so that older Jennifer can take it out and pay taxes at whatever rate is applicable then." She perceives not paying taxes now on that $10,000 as a benefit.

In her 401(k), Jennifer has a limited choice of ten, twenty, or maybe fifty different investments out of a world of thousands of investments. Someone at ABC Corporation, typically the business owner or the chief financial officer (CFO), has chosen this limited menu of mutual funds. Jennifer has no input regarding what investment choices are made available in her 401(k). She also has no idea why the investment choices in her 401(k) were selected over other choices. They may be independently rated as excellent choices. They may be the choices of the CFO's brother who's in the financial industry and receives commission on the 401(k) assets. They may be the most convenient choices and come with exorbitant fees. Like Jennifer, you have no influence over your 401(k) choices.

Let's say Jennifer is satisfied with her 401(k) investment choices until the CFO leaves and the new CFO at ABC

Corporation changes the 401(k) plan. Of course, Jennifer wasn't asked her opinion before the change. Now she's not happy with the new choices and wants her $10,000 investment back.

Well, as soon as Jennifer put that $10,000 in her traditional 401(k), she took the IRS deal, and now she can't take her money out until she's age fifty-nine and a half without incurring a penalty. If she pulls it out of the traditional 401(k), her $10,000 is subject to income tax in the year she takes it out. On top of that, she must pay a 10 percent IRS penalty.

Between ages fifty-nine and a half and seventy and a half, Jennifer can take as much money as she would like penalty-free (though her withdrawals are still subject to income tax). I call these eleven years "magical," because they are the only years in which the government does not use penalties to suppress your choices of how you spend your own money.

After Jennifer reaches age seventy and a half, the IRS will force her to take out money every year from her traditional 401(k) and traditional IRA savings. This amount is referred to as a *Required Minimum Distribution*, or *RMD*. If Jennifer's RMD in a given year is $20,000, but she does not withdraw this amount, she will pay a hefty penalty of 50 percent, or $10,000, for not playing by the IRS rules.

To sum up, here's what Jennifer did when she decided to put $10,000 in her traditional 401(k):

- She ceded control of her investment options to her employer.
- She gave the IRS control of how she may use her money for all but eleven years of her life.
- She predicted tax rates will be lower for her in the future; otherwise, she will pay more income taxes on her $10,000 in the future than she would have today. The IRS will determine how much she gets to keep after income taxes.
- She retained all of the investment risk. If her investments fail, the IRS doesn't allow her to deduct losses. The more her investments succeed, the greater share the IRS will likely take in income taxes.

I am not against contributing to traditional 401(k) plans whatsoever. However, I've just applied critical thinking to the decision. How does that strike you? You may end up taking the same action, contributing to your traditional 401(k), but you will likely be more confident about your decision because you've confronted the limitations and not just blindly accepted the benefits!

YOU MAY PAY TAX ON THE SEEDS, NOT ON THE HARVEST

We've learned—perhaps from Uncle Joe, the Internet, or a financial advisor—that putting money in a tax-deferred account is a good thing to do. But remember, there are no good or bad financial products or strategies; there is only what's right for your situation.

When you contribute to a pretax account, such as a traditional IRA, a traditional 401(k), or a 403(b) for public or nonprofit employees, those contributions are the seeds that you hope will grow into a big pile of money that you'll harvest during retirement. The IRS says, when you contribute to one of these accounts, it's not going to tax you on these seeds (tax-deductible contributions).

Over several decades, those seeds hopefully blossom into a big, abundant harvest represented as a large account value. Now you must pay taxes on the harvest. That's right—every dollar withdrawn (harvested) from your account is subject to income taxes at the rate applicable to you in the year you withdraw the money. If you were a farmer, buying seeds might not be cheap, but the cost of those seeds would not be nearly as expensive as the value of your crops. Would you rather pay tax on the seeds or on the harvest? Think about it.

In contrast, with a *tax-free* account, such as a Roth IRA

or a Roth 401(k), you pay tax on the seeds and not the harvest. If you get the taxes out of the way, those seeds literally grow tax-free, not tax-deferred. You have made a very different deal with the IRS.

- You don't have to pay taxes on the harvest. Distributions are income-tax-free, including all the growth earned over many years.
- You do have to pay a 10 percent penalty on any growth withdrawn prior to age fifty-nine and a half.
- You can make withdrawals with no negative tax impact, even if tax rates increase in the future.
- If you contribute to a Roth 401(k), you still cede control of investment choices to your employer.
- You do not have a Required Minimum Distribution (RMD) at seventy and a half or ever.

So, what is the best choice for you? It depends. Your employer may not offer a Roth 401(k), and if this is the case, then push them to offer one! The IRS sets income limitations that might prohibit you from contributing to a Roth IRA.

Here's one way to decide if a tax-deferred account makes sense for you. Ask yourself these two questions:

- In the future, do I believe my income-tax rates will go up, go down, or stay the same?

- If I believe they will go up, why would I defer paying taxes today, when I believe the rate is lower, and choose to pay taxes in the future, when I think tax rates will be higher?

"Ah," you may be saying, "but I will be in a lower tax bracket when I retire." Sounds familiar, but let's keep our critical thinking hat on! Actually, the more successful you are at saving money, the higher your income may be in retirement, which means that your taxes may not be lower. And even if you are solidly in the middle of the road income-wise, other circumstances may cause your taxes to be the same, if not higher. Let's see what happens to Sally and Jim.

Sally and Jim are married and have a gross household income of $96,000. They take the standard deductions and exemptions on their tax return, which means their taxable income is approximately $75,000 in round numbers. In 2017, if you are married filing jointly and your taxable income is between $18,650 and $75,900, you are in the 15 percent tax bracket. The majority of the employed American public falls into this category. (In future years, specific numbers will change, but this IRS income-tax structure has been in place for many decades, so the concept likely will not change.)

Now Sally and Jim decide to retire. Between Social Security and any retirement accounts they have, whether in a pension (which is becoming less common) or a traditional 401(k) or similar plan, they have a retirement income of $50,000, which means their taxable income might be approximately $29,000. Their income in retirement is nearly half of their income when employed, yet they are in the same tax bracket of 15 percent. In this example, they deferred money subject to income tax at 15 percent while they were working, and when they take it out in retirement, it's still subject to the same 15 percent tax rate.

What if tax rates increased? Might the IRS increase the tax rate from 15 percent to 18 percent or more? You might believe this is more possible than the IRS reducing the 15 percent tax bracket to 12 percent or less. Under the increasing tax rate scenario, it's not in Sally's and Jim's best interests to defer paying 15 percent in taxes while they are working and instead pay 18 percent when they make withdrawals from their IRA/401(k) accounts in retirement.

Let's look at another example that doesn't involve predicting whether tax rates go up or down. If you are married, what is the likelihood that either you or your spouse will die first? Pretty good huh? Like 100 percent probable, right? Unless you and your beloved spouse die simultaneously in your sleep holding hands, it is much more likely that either you or your spouse will be a widow or widower at some point. Let's see what might happen to Sally and Jim in this situation.

Sadly, Jim dies. Beginning with the year after Jim's death, Sally now must file as a single person. In 2017, the 15 percent bracket for a single filer is between $9,326 and $37,950. This means that every dollar of taxable income over $37,950 is taxed at a minimum of 25 percent, not the 15 percent applicable while Jim was alive. You are reading this correctly! For many couples the tax rate on the surviving spouse may increase substantially when the first spouse dies. Therefore, even if IRS tax rates don't change, deferring taxes in traditional 401(k) and traditional IRA accounts may lead to much higher taxation simply because you or your spouse died, which is certain to happen!

This is the biggest jump in our marginal tax system—from the 15 percent bracket to the 25 percent bracket. Even if Sally's taxable income, after Jim passed, is reduced to $40,000, she will still pay higher taxes, rather than lower taxes, on her retirement withdrawals than she would have paid on this money when she and Jim were working.

THE MAGICAL ELEVEN YEARS

When your money is in a traditional 401(k) or traditional

IRA, you have that magical eleven years when you can choose for yourself how much to withdraw penalty-free. You've established a habit of saving, and you've been socking money away in these accounts for decades. Now you're ready to retire, and you are in that eleven-year window. The money is yours to spend!

However, all too often I see people who hesitate to take money out of their tax-deferred retirement account because they think, "Oh my gosh, if I do, it's all going to be taxable." But ask yourself, "Why am I keeping the money in my traditional 401(k) or traditional IRA?" If it's a tax-deferred account, the money is going to be taxable whenever you withdraw it. If you die with $1 million in an IRA and your child inherits it, they will not get the $1 million—they will get the $1 million minus taxes due.

Remember, *this is about you*. It's about what *you* want your money to do for *you*. If you leave that money in your tax-deferred account until you are age seventy and a half, you are going to be required to take a minimum amount and pay taxes on it every year for the rest of your life. But then you will be eleven years older and perhaps not as able as you would have been to buy that RV and drive across the country, or take an Alaskan cruise, or buy a sports car, or whatever you want to do for you.

I'm not suggesting you take the money out before age fifty-nine and a half if you can avoid it, because you'll incur the 10 percent penalty, plus taxes due. I am suggesting you think about how to make your money support your fun and lifestyle with the minimum tax burden over time.

If you believe taxes are going to go up in your lifetime, and you're not willing to have the use of your money controlled so much by the IRS, perhaps you'll want to consider alternative ways to save and invest for retirement.

USE TAX LAW TO YOUR ADVANTAGE

There are many ways to make the tax laws work for you when considering how to save for retirement. I've outlined three below.

TAKE THE COMPANY MATCH

By all means, if your company offers to match your contribution to a traditional or Roth 401(k), you'll likely benefit by taking this deal. This is free money contributed by your employer. If the ABC Corporation agrees to match the first 3 percent of what Jennifer puts in her 401(k), Jennifer doubles her contribution if she commits to saving 3 percent of her salary. But with a traditional IRA, 401(k), or 403(b), anything over the match means that Jennifer has decided to defer paying taxes on her money. As we have demonstrated, this strategy may or may not benefit Jennifer depending on future tax rates and whether she is married or single.

BECOME A CORPORATION OF ONE

In our next example, Jennifer has had a change of heart. She's decided to leave ABC Corporation and strike out on her own as a consultant. Many more Americans are choosing to become self-employed these days. Like me, they may discover their latent entrepreneurial talent!

After a slow start, Jennifer has a good year, making the same $100,000 she had made as a salaried employee. When she files her taxes, if she claims the entire amount as income, all $100,000 is now subject to a 15.3 percent self-employment tax. This covers the full share of her Federal Insurance Contributions Act (FICA) tax, imposed on both employees and employers to fund Social Security and Medicare. When Jennifer was an employee, ABC Corporation would have paid half that amount—7.65 percent—and the other half would have been deducted from Jennifer's paycheck. As a consultant, though, Jennifer is on the hook for the whole amount.

However, Jennifer has a choice. She can decide to incorporate. Though it's beyond the scope of this book to discuss the legal ramifications of incorporating, the potential tax implications are worth a look.

After incorporating, Jennifer can choose to pay herself a salary of, say, $25,000, all of which is subject to self-employment tax. The IRS provides latitude in establishing a salary, because business income can fluctuate from year to year, sometimes substantially so. The other $75,000 is considered excess profit, which is subject to state and federal taxes but not self-employment tax. If Jennifer is not paying 15.3 percent on $75,000, she has just saved more than $11,000, which she could use to fund a retirement account.

Either as an employee or as an unincorporated self-employed individual, Jennifer is limited to what she can contribute to an IRA, whether it's traditional or Roth. If she is younger than age fifty, she can contribute no more than $5,500 a year. At age fifty and beyond, she can contribute $6,500 a year, provided she has earned income equal to or greater than her contribution.

As the head of a corporation, however, Jennifer can create her own 401(k). Now she gets to decide what funds to invest in, because it's her plan! And she can contribute $18,000 per year to a 401(k), plus an additional $6,000 if she has had her fiftieth birthday. She may also choose to establish a traditional or Roth 401(k) or both. Being your own boss has both tax benefits and limitations, and it pays to understand how to make the tax code work for you.

There is one important caveat, though. Jennifer's Social Security payment will be based on what she pays into the system. In our example, if Jennifer pays FICA tax only on $25,000, rather than on $100,000, her contribution to the Social Security system is reduced substantially. But this still might be a good trade for Jennifer. When she dies, it doesn't matter how much she has paid into the Social Security system; there is no accumulated principal that may be passed on to her heirs, since anything that did not go to her remains in Social Security for others. However, if Jennifer has instead invested the more than $11,000 she gained by taking a lower salary, she may leave that to anyone she chooses.

CHOOSE TO DIVERSIFY

It's not unusual for me to work with successful executives who have done very well and saved $2 million or more for their retirement, but it's nearly all in their 401(k)s. Now their lifestyle is affected by what the tax rate is throughout retirement. If you're in this situation and you're pulling $100,000 a year out of a tax-deferred 401(k), whether tax rates go up or down can affect how much you can spend. There's no flexibility, and that's not ideal.

When you are working for a company and choose to put your retirement nest egg in the company's traditional 401(k), you may feel that the number of funds from which you can choose—whether it's twenty or fifty—is more than enough. Perhaps you find it confusing to have even that many options.

If you choose to save money outside of the 401(k), however, you have all the choices in the 401(k) and literally thousands of others. All other things being equal, you will benefit from more choices. If you have an affinity for investing, and/or you are working with a competent financial advisor, you will likely benefit more outside of the limited menu than you will inside that menu.

Ideally, when you retire, you will have different buckets of money, each of which is taxed differently. Let's say you have one bucket of money in which you paid no taxes along the way, but it's taxable when you take it out. You have another bucket that has grown tax-free and is tax-free when you take money out. You may have a third bucket of money where you saved and invested money outside of retirement accounts altogether!

Now you can make flexible distribution decisions. For

example, if income-tax rates are high in a particular year, but you want some money to support your fun and lifestyle, you might take from the tax-free bucket. If tax rates are lower in another year, you might choose to take money from the tax-deferred bucket at reduced tax rates while you can.

Ultimately, you might think of diversifying your exposure to the tax code in much the same way as you diversify when you invest.

PLAN NOW TO SAVE TIME AND MONEY LATER

This entire chapter has focused on the tax implications of the investment choices you make. The message is simple: the more forward-thinking you are about these decisions, the more time and less frustration you will have as April 15 approaches each year. Taking a box full of receipts to your accountant and crossing your fingers is no way to ensure that you are making the best use of your money from a tax perspective! Find a financial planning firm that integrates tax planning with investment planning; see chapter 16 for more information about how to choose the advisor who is right for you.

USE YOUR CRITICAL-THINKING SKILLS

For any of the decisions we've discussed, you'll want to

use the critical-thinking skills we highlighted previously. Ask yourself, "What do I want my money to do for me?" Consider your deal breakers. If having full control of your retirement funds for only eleven years is a deal breaker, a traditional tax-deferred retirement account may not be the best choice for all or some of your savings.

Most importantly, ask yourself, "What if I did the exact opposite?" What if you didn't contribute to a 401(k) beyond the company match? Remember, the key is the discipline to save. If you accumulate money in accounts without restrictions, you may use your money at any age to do whatever you want, from starting your own business to sailing around the world. This is your life, and *life isn't lived on a spreadsheet*. In the next chapter, we'll examine how you may accumulate money tax-free over the course of your life, but you'll need to bring your critical-thinking skills with you!

LIFE INSURANCE: A VERY POWERFUL TOOL DESPITE MAXIMUM BIAS

Everyone seems to want outcomes like tax-free growth and a large pot of money that's guaranteed from investment risk when they retire.

What are the odds you will die? We know it's 100 percent, and, therefore, life insurance is the only insurance guaranteed to pay benefits.[1] What are those benefits? Tax-free cash, often when the people you care for the most need it, after your death.

---

1   Guarantees provided are based on the claims-paying ability of the issuing company.

Life insurance is a unique and powerful financial tool in which you give an insurance company a relatively small amount of money to create a very large pile of money payable when you die. There is no other financial tool that can do this. For some financial objectives, life insurance is the only solution. In my experience, life insurance also incites more consumer and advisor bias than any other financial product or strategy. Let's examine why and learn more about this enigmatic product!

BIG BAGS OF TAX-FREE CASH

People often love the outcomes that a life insurance policy may provide. Regardless of the type of life insurance you choose, when you die, the policy becomes a bag of tax-free cash for your family, charity, or whomever you choose. In the IRS tax code, life insurance has unique benefits relative to other financial tools.

Your situation may be best served by a temporary or "term" life insurance policy, which is primarily designed for your unexpected death within a chosen time frame or "term" of years. If you die during the term of your policy, the death benefit is paid. If you do not die during that term, there is no other financial benefit.

Your situation may be best served by a permanent life

insurance policy, which is designed to pay economic benefits while you live and regardless of when you die because the policy does not end until you do. A permanent life insurance policy accumulates cash value that may grow tax-free with very few restrictions.

Previously, we covered Roth IRAs and Roth 401(k)s, which provide tax-free growth if you qualify. There are many life insurance policies that provide tax-free growth as well. Believe it or not, tax-free growth is not always in your best interest if the limitations attached to that benefit are incompatible with your objectives.

However, why would anyone dismiss the possibility of tax-free cash growth by owning a life insurance policy without any due diligence? You have probably already guessed the answer! Bias. Sometimes, there's an unhinged bias about this product.

We referred earlier to making deals with the IRS. Let's examine the deal you may make by owning certain permanent life insurance policies.

- Your premiums may accumulate cash on a tax-free basis without IRS restrictions or penalties, regardless of when you choose to use your own money. You can access the money prior to age fifty-nine and a half, and the IRS does not require you to take money out of your life insurance policy at seventy and a half or any age. You can use your money to start a business without using 401(k) or IRA money and having to pay IRS penalties. While you are living, your cash value may pay for a variety of objectives and contribute to a successful retirement for you and your family.

- If you become permanently disabled and have a disability rider on your life policy,[2] the insurance company adds to your cash value as if you were making the premium payments yourself! Think about this. If you become permanently disabled, your cash accumulation continues. No investment plan, 401(k), or IRA will do that for you.

- If you die prior to accumulating your retirement nest egg, the life policy death benefit, in effect, accelerates your savings by paying a lump sum of tax-free cash. The cash death benefits help keep your family in your home when you die and maintain the standard of living you want for them.

Life insurance provides tax-free growth, tax-free access, and tax-free money when you pass away, whether you die at age thirty-two in an accident or peacefully in your sleep when you're 110 years old. Live, become disabled, or

---

2   Riders are available for an additional fee; some riders may not be available in all states.

die—a permanent life insurance policy provides tremendous security and benefits to complement your investment portfolio and other financial planning.

One way or another, life insurance is always going to pay off! You buy homeowner's insurance, but you don't know that your house is going to burn down. You buy car insurance, but you don't know that you are going to be involved in an accident. But you do know, with certainty, that you are going to die.

Accumulating big, fat bags of tax-free cash seems like a no-brainer to me. But even in the financial services industry, agents and advisors often fall into one of two camps. Some say permanent life insurance is "horrible," while others say it's "great." They're both wrong. It depends on your specific facts and objectives.

But there is a catch. You knew it was coming, didn't you? You must be healthy enough to qualify for life insurance. Not everyone who wants life insurance will qualify.

However, if you can qualify, I believe life insurance should have a role in your financial plan. You may leverage the certainty of your death and spend other assets with more freedom! Let's examine where your biases might get in the way of making the decision about life insurance that's best for you.

DON'T BLAME THE PERSON FOR THE PRODUCT

Insurance companies make insurance products the way that Ford makes cars. Also, much as your car salesperson does, your life insurance salesperson makes his or her money on commission.

Buying life insurance is a transaction between a consumer and an agent or broker. The compensation received by the agent or broker is a commission, paid by the insurance company when the policy is put in force. This commission varies, but it is generally between 60 percent and 100 percent of the first-year policy premium. This commission percentage is similar whether the life insurance is "term" or "permanent." The insurance company pays the commission to the broker. The consumer does not pay the commission.

Buying life insurance may be fraught with uncertainty. To begin with, you're already uncomfortable because nobody wants to think about dying. Then you sit down with an agent or independent broker who receives a commission if you buy a policy but no compensation if you don't. Commission-based compensation may lead to behavior and recommendations that are not in your best interest.

Commission-based compensation is not bad, particularly if there is full understanding and disclosure provided to the consumer. However, this commission-based structure adds tremendous bias about the product in a consumer's mind. Additionally, the product is often sold by agents or brokers who may not have comprehensive experience, licensing, a financial planning background, or significant knowledge of the various types of life insurance policies and how they differ from one another.

On top of this, maybe you don't understand what life insurance does or what type is right for you. The way life insurance works is likely unfamiliar to you, and your agent or broker may not know that much about it either. But you know they stand to gain if you buy. So, if you begin to feel that the process of buying insurance has become uncomfortable or even adversarial, you may attach these negative feelings to the product rather than to the person and their process for selling the life insurance policy.

But you have a choice, because *this is about your life*. If you want to know more about life insurance, or you think life insurance may be worth more due diligence on your part, you might seek the knowledge of an experienced advisor with whom you are comfortable asking candid questions. You should never feel rushed to make any significant financial decisions, and purchasing life insurance qualifies.

IF YOU LIKE BENEFITS AT WORK, YOU'LL REALLY LIKE BENEFITS AT HOME

Everyone loves benefits. When you or your grown child gets a job, one of the first things you ask is, "How are the benefits?" Company benefits often include health insurance, life insurance, disability insurance, and a retirement plan.

This is one of the strangest aspects of financial planning. Employees typically love insurance and retirement savings benefits and choose careers and jobs based on them. Yet, many people do not choose to purchase these same benefits themselves even when the benefits may be tailored to their best interests!

When you pay your premiums into a permanent life insurance policy, you're building cash equity within the life insurance policy, similar to building equity in your home. Over the long term, you may have far more cash in the policy than the premium you put in, while owning insurance benefits as well. This cash growth is tax-free, and the insurance benefits may cover life, disability, and/or long-term care needs.

This is such a paradox. People want benefits but often don't buy insurance, even though benefits equal insurance and are critical to quality financial planning.

In most industries, life insurance included, marketing is driven toward the masses. The thought is, "How can we connect with the consumer and motivate a buying decision?" Information often is generic and may not apply to your unique situation.

That's why you have both a right and a responsibility to make thoughtful decisions. Always remember that money is just a medium of exchange; its sole purpose is to help you get what you want out of life.

Start with your desired outcomes in mind, and work backward. Set aside bias, and apply critical thinking about how a life insurance policy might contribute toward your desired outcomes. What benefits are in your best interest, and what limitations can you live with or are deal breakers?

Unlike your 401(k) and other retirement plans, permanent life insurance is not a short-term cash accumulation strategy. Many of the benefits that life insurance provides are included in other products or employment benefits, so they are not unfamiliar.

You may be uncomfortable thinking about dying, but you may be equally uncomfortable, if not more so, thinking about being very much alive but no longer able to care for yourself. We'll examine long-term care insurance in the next chapter.

LONG-TERM CARE INSURANCE: A BAD VISUAL AND BIAS

The perfect time to buy long-term care insurance is at least one day before you cannot buy it.

As with most types of insurance, to purchase long-term care insurance, you must prove that you don't need it, at least on the day you want to buy it. Furthermore, because *life isn't lived on a spreadsheet*, you don't know the exact day when you will no longer qualify. In this chapter, we'll examine why long-term care insurance may be an important part of your financial plan, even though the choice is loaded with emotion and bias.

YOU ARE GOING TO RECEIVE LONG-TERM CARE FROM SOMEONE

We don't want to think about not being able to take care of ourselves; we all want to be independent right up to the moment this freedom is taken away from us. There may come a day when you don't remember your own name, despite knowing it the previous day.

I've heard many people say that if their health declines to the point of needing long-term nursing care, "just shoot me." Well, that's a silly response, even if someone were willing to risk jail to do this for you.

It's almost easier to think about dying, because then the discussion is around what you want your financial legacy to be—how much you want to leave to your children or to charity. That's a positive vision of the future, even if it's someone else's future.

Long-term care insurance pays off when you are no longer physically able to care for yourself. When you can't perform two of six activities of daily living (ADLs)—eating, bathing, dressing, toileting, transferring (walking), and continence—this will trigger your policy benefits. And no one wants to imagine that they can't walk themselves to the bathroom or lift a spoon to their mouth. This is simply a nightmare vision for many people.

Modern medicine is keeping us alive longer. Whether it's providing us with quality of life is debatable. Your mind or body may wear out while you remain alive. Who will care for you when you can no longer care for yourself? Perhaps your spouse or your kids? They may have good intentions, but do they have the energy and expertise to care for you around the clock?

Your need for long-term care is not something you have control over. If your health declines to the point that you cannot care for yourself, someone or some facility must care for you. So how are you going to pay for this care? You do have some choices in how to answer this question.

PAY WITH YOUR MONEY OR SOMEONE ELSE'S MONEY?

Providing care 24/7 is expensive. Depending on where you live, a three-year stay in a long-term care facility can cost upward of $250,000. Even if you had the money to cover this, wouldn't you rather leave it to your children or your favorite charity? Do you want to pay these costs with your money, or would you rather use someone else's money?

A long-term care insurance policy is simply a way to set aside a relatively small amount of money to create a huge benefit when you need it. And *you* get to make this choice.

Even if you are wealthy, long-term care can be an asset-protection tool.

Here's how it works.

You buy a monthly benefit amount—maybe it's $2,000 a month or maybe it's $10,000 a month. The larger the benefit monthly, the more expensive the policy premium is. Let's say you choose a $5,000-a-month benefit, or $60,000 a year. You can elect to buy a benefit for a time frame you specify, whether it's for two years, for five years, or for a lifetime. The longer the guaranteed time frame, the more expensive the policy is.

You can also choose to add an inflation rider if you are concerned that $60,000 might not go very far when you need it in the future. You may add this rider allowing your benefit to grow by a certain percentage—say, by 3 percent or 5 percent—every year. Of course, any choice that adds benefit also adds cost.

Some long-term care policies may include a return-of-premium rider. Let's say you paid a premium of $4,000 a year for twenty years, for a total of $80,000, but you never triggered the benefit, which is a good thing! Maybe you remain healthy to a ripe old age and pass away peacefully in your sleep. With the return-of-premium rider, your beneficiaries get the $80,000 back.

In that scenario, you didn't earn interest on the money, so that's an opportunity cost. But had you needed the insurance, you would have been still able to pass on the bulk of your estate to your family, so not earning interest may not be a deal breaker for you. Always remember, *this is about what you want your money to do for you.* Ask questions until you feel you have all the facts necessary for a thoughtful decision.

One important fact to keep in mind is this: if you need long-term care, that means you're not dead. You're still breathing, which means you're still receiving Social Security and pension income, if applicable. This is important to your long-term care decision in the context of overall financial planning.

Let's say the average cost of long-term care (not the insurance) in your area is $7,000 a month. You might think you need a policy that pays a $7,000-a-month benefit. But if you have a Social Security check of $2,000 a month, why not get a long-term care policy that covers just the difference of $5,000 a month? Therefore, you are not overpaying for benefits covered in other ways. Good financial planning is individualized to your situation. You may want a policy that covers some but not all the risk.

HAVE YOUR CAKE AND EAT IT, TOO

What if you do want long-term care insurance, but you don't want to pay an annual premium? There's an interesting option called asset-based long-term care, which is a hybrid life insurance and long-term care policy.

Imagine yourself with $100,000 in cash. Let's say you don't want to risk that money in the stock market, and you are concerned about the financial risk associated with a long-term care stay. You put $100,000 into an asset-based long-term care policy. This creates three buckets of money.

The first bucket is the cash bucket. The $100,000 you invest may be liquid for you to withdraw whenever you choose. If you change your mind in three weeks or in three years, you may take your $100,000 back and move on with your life. No questions asked. The cash is still there for you to use.

The second bucket of money is the life insurance bucket. You put $100,000 into the policy, and, if you die before needing long-term care, or before withdrawing the cash, your heirs will inherit more than your $100,000, and the extra cash is income-tax-free as a life insurance benefit.

The third bucket of money, which would be the main driver of this purchase decision, is the long-term care insurance bucket. This bucket may leverage your $100,000 deposit to create $300,000 or more. If, at some point, you need long-term care, you now have $300,000, not $100,000, to spend toward that care. This leveraged benefit may protect you from having to spend other savings and investments.

Many people like this option because it's simple and clean. You have control of your money if you change your mind. Because it's a one-time, lump-sum payment, it's not possible for there to be any future rate increases, and there are no monthly or annual premiums to be paid.

A potential downside is the need to park what may be a significant amount of your assets in the policy. But let's look at that through the lens of critical thinking.

You could have taken that same $100,000 and put it in a certificate of deposit (CD) or a money market account at your bank. But in a low-interest environment, those accounts may pay only half a percent. That's $500 in a year on your $100,000.

If you don't want to put your $100,000 at risk, rather than earning half a percent at the bank, you can put it in an asset-based long-term care policy. In return for giving up the $500 a year in potential interest, you gain life insurance and long-term care benefits.

Remember, too, that these assets are liquid. If years from now the local bank is paying 5 percent on their CDs like they were in years past, you could earn $5,000 a year on your $100,000 investment. Then, if you want to take the money out of your asset-based long-term care policy and put it in a CD, you may do so and give up your benefits in exchange for higher interest. It's flexible. That doesn't mean it's better or worse than another insurance policy or investment. It just means this is one more tool you have at your disposal, should you decide it's right for you.

Just as you might not be familiar with how long-term care insurance works, you may not understand what an annuity is. Or worse, you may have formed an impression about annuities based on misinformation or another source of bias. We'll examine annuities and the bias that surrounds them in the next chapter.

ANNUITIES: DON'T BE OLD, SANE, AND BROKE!

We've all been young, sane, and broke and lived to tell about it.

If you are old and broke, but your mind fails, you may not understand the difficult situation you are in.

The absolute scariest situation is to be old, sane, and broke. That's a scary place to be. You know you need money, but you can't go back to work. And you are fully aware of your dire situation.

Consumers, brokers, and advisors alike often say that annuities are complicated. The fact is annuities are not complicated, but they are unfamiliar to many and, therefore, misunderstood.

Annuities are most commonly distributed through financial professionals on a commission basis. This may lead a financial professional to steer you toward a sale, which often creates bias. You should be entirely focused on your own best interests and determine what annuities do and what they don't do toward meeting your desired financial outcomes. Annuities are commonplace in retirement planning, but as with insurance benefits, people often don't seek to buy them on their own.

INCOME FOR LIFE

"Annuity" is simply a fancy word for regular income payments over time. Guaranteed income is something people universally love. Social Security income is annuity income. If you have pension income, that is annuity income. Everybody loves getting their Social Security or pension check every month. People almost lose their minds if a politician attempts to discuss reducing Social Security benefits! So here is where we see mass bias at play. People love the benefit of guaranteed income for life, yet they often don't purchase that benefit privately.

Unlike life and long-term care insurance, you do not have

to qualify medically to receive guaranteed income for the rest of your life, regardless of how long you live. Everyone may add guaranteed income benefits in their financial planning. So why do people say annuities are bad? Yes, you guessed it! Bias.

Annuities are not good or bad. Annuities are the only financial tool available to you that guarantee lifetime income. No investment portfolio can meet that objective. Does that mean annuities are better than investment portfolios? Absolutely not, but it may mean you should do your due diligence, which may lead to a combination of strategies involving both investments and annuities.

You can't control what the government does with Social Security or what your company does with your pension. Many companies have dropped traditional pensions altogether. By using private annuities, you may tailor your income benefits precisely to your objectives.

FIXED ANNUITIES ARE NOT A FREE LUNCH!

We all know there is no such thing as a free lunch.

Other than putting your money in a savings account, if you want guaranteed principal, you may have only three options. You can get a federal government bond, a bank certificate of deposit (CD), or a fixed annuity from an insurance company. You are likely familiar with federal government bonds and CDs. Fixed annuities may be unfamiliar to you, but their features are remarkably similar to bonds and CDs.

First, each of the three comes with guarantees. The United States government guarantees the principal on a government bond. As long as our government survives, which is a pretty sure bet, a federal government bond may be the lowest-risk place on the planet to put your money.

The bank that holds your CD guarantees your principal. If your bank fails, a stronger bank may acquire your struggling bank and guarantee your principal. This is the free market at work. Finally, if your bank fails without being bailed out, your last line of defense is the Federal Deposit Insurance Corporation (FDIC), which insures each deposit account for up to $250,000.

A fixed annuity is similar, except that it is an insurance industry product, not a banking industry product. The insurance company with whom you invest your money guarantees the principal of your fixed annuity. If your insurance company struggles, the free market may kick in, and a stronger insurance company may acquire your insurance company and guarantee your fixed annuity.

What happens if that insurance company goes belly up? To do business in any state, the insurance company has to pay into a state guaranty fund that may provide each annuity owner a certain amount of protection, which ranges from state to state, currently between $100,000 and $500,000. A fixed annuity is not FDIC insured or backed by any federal government agency.

A fixed annuity shares other characteristics with both a federal government bond and a CD. None of these products has a share price, nor do they pay dividends. Each of these financial instruments pays interest, which is subject to ordinary income-tax rates.

Also, there are no internal fees attached to a federal government bond, a CD, or the clear majority of fixed annuities. None. If you put $100,000 in a fixed annuity, CD, or government bond, that whole $100,000 begins earning interest.

You have guaranteed principal, no investment risk, and no fees. Well, that sounds like a free lunch! There is no free lunch. You are exchanging some of your liquidity for a higher interest rate or other benefits.

You get to choose your interest rate from among several options offered by the insurance company or the bank;

however, you give up some liquidity. For example, you will likely get a higher rate of return on a five-year CD than on a three-year CD, and a higher rate on a three-year CD than on a one-year CD.

In return for letting the bank use your money for a longer period of time, they sweeten the deal for you. The same is typically true for a federal government bond or a fixed annuity. The bank or insurance company doesn't charge you a fee, but they profit by using your money during the time frame for which you committed.

So, why might you choose a fixed annuity versus similar alternatives? This is the type of question you should be asking.

First, you may have more liquidity with a fixed annuity than a bank CD. Anytime you are going to commit your money for a specified period of time, whether for one year or twenty years, you want to be as certain as you can be that you won't need it. With a CD, you may receive interest during the time frame you committed to, but you will pay a penalty for touching the principal before the time frame is completed.

In contrast, a fixed annuity typically offers a certain percentage of penalty-free liquidity exceeding the interest rate. For example, if you invest $100,000 in a CD paying 3 percent interest, you get $3,000 a year in interest. With a fixed annuity that offers 3 percent interest, you will likely have 10 percent penalty-free liquidity; therefore, you have access to 10 percent of your principal, or $10,000. This includes the $3,000 in interest and an additional $7,000 if you want it. All other things being equal, there may be more liquidity in a fixed annuity than in a CD.

Because a fixed annuity is an insurance company product, there are typically additional benefits for your heirs. With a fixed annuity, the surrender penalty—the penalty for cashing in prior to the term you selected—is waived when you die. Your heirs may have access to 100 percent of the value, even if you die before the term is up. In contrast, if you have a bond or a CD, your heirs may have to decide whether to cash in and pay the penalty or wait till the term has run its course.

To sum up, there are very minor differences between a federal government bond, a CD, and a fixed annuity. I make this point because very few people are biased against bonds or CDs. A person may not choose a bond or a CD, but they are not typically blinded by bias about those products. However, fixed annuity bias is more common. What are people afraid of? Simply apply critical thinking and do your due diligence. Let's examine where the bias comes from.

THE COMMISSION CONFLICT

An annuity is an insurance company product, and as we saw with life insurance and long-term care insurance, individuals and firms that sell annuities are paid commission. By contrast, there are typically no commissions paid on a CD. The bank is not a charity, however. The bank has already figured its overhead and expenses into the interest rate it can pay you. Believe me, the bank makes plenty of money from offering CDs.

Even when the insurance carrier pays 100 percent of the commission to the agent or broker (the client pays zero percent), a potential conflict of interest exists because there is no commission if you don't buy. Whether the fixed annuity is in your best interest or not, the insurance company will pay the same commission. Insurance companies review every application to determine client suitability, but they are not typically aware of your overall financial situation and objectives. The commission has nothing to do with what the product contributes toward achieving your objectives. Don't be distracted by what commission may be paid. Focus on your best interests, not the agent's or broker's! Consider the benefits and limitations that apply to you. What does the strategy do or not do for you?

A HORSE OF A VERY DIFFERENT COLOR

To this point, everything I've described applies to a fixed annuity. A variable annuity has investment risk. Your principal is not guaranteed with a variable annuity as it is with a fixed annuity.

You have a limited menu of investment options that may rise and fall with the stock and bond markets. A variable annuity also has significant fees and expenses as compared to a fixed annuity, which does not typically have any fees or expenses.

Remember, however, that there is no good or bad financial product; *there is only the choice that's right for you.* A variable annuity has one unique feature that might make it a good choice for the right person in the right situation. When you die, your heirs will typically inherit 100 percent of what you put into the annuity, less any withdrawals, regardless of its current market value. So, if your variable annuity fails as an investment and you die during this time, your beneficiary will receive 100 percent of your contributions, less withdrawals, or the current market value, whichever is larger.

Say you put $100,000 in a typical variable annuity, which, because of market fluctuations, ends up only worth $50,000 when you die. Your heirs are entitled to the full

$100,000, provided you didn't make any withdrawals. That's unlike a 401(k) or individual stocks, where if you lose, you lose, and so do your heirs.

Whom might this benefit? Recently, I helped a client who had retired after being diagnosed with cancer. He wanted to reinvest a sizable 401(k), and we considered all the options. He wanted the money to grow, so he was willing to take investment risk. But he knew that if he put his money in the market directly and it lost value, he would be leaving his wife less than he had accumulated in his 401(k). He wanted to take investment risk, but also guarantee the amount payable to his wife if he died from cancer. A variable annuity is the only investment on the planet that can provide investment risk/opportunity and a guaranteed death benefit.

With the variable annuity, the fees and expenses were not deal breakers, because this client was uninsurable and no other financial instrument could provide the outcome he desired. He knew that his wife would get no less—and possibly more—than his original investment. Given his cancer diagnosis, this made the most sense for him. (I'm happy to report that he beat the odds and is enjoying his retirement.)

Just remember, however, that the only guaranteed principal in a variable annuity is if you die. If you're alive and well, and your $100,000 annuity ends up being worth only $50,000, you've got $50,000 to spend. Period. You've still lost the money, like losses in a mutual fund, but you're likely paying higher fees and expenses in the variable annuity based on the additional benefits, which lowers your return. It is not unusual for variable annuity fees to exceed 3 percent annually.

IT'S ALL ABOUT YOU

If you take one thing away from this book, remember that the goal of financial planning is *what you want your money to do for you.* To be a savvy consumer of financial products and services, you must apply critical thinking to any decisions you make. Hold your biases up to the light of day. Weigh your options, including the option of doing the exact opposite of what is being recommended. Choose a financial advisor who will both challenge and respect you.

When you go into these decisions with an open and inquisitive mind, you may begin challenging yourself. In the next chapter, we'll look at why it might be a good idea to question the conventional wisdom that everyone should own their own home. Hang on tight!

BUY OR RENT, IT'S THE SAME HOUSE

You have to live somewhere, but you don't have to own where you live.

Buying a home to live in is not an investment. It's about where you want to live, what schools you want your children to attend, and even what you want your house to say about you (yes, ego may play a role in home buying). But unless you get really lucky, owning a home is a lousy investment. Forget what your parents or Uncle Bill told you. There are plenty of good reasons to buy a house, but making money is not one of them. Let's explore this further.

WHAT'S MONEY GOT TO DO WITH IT?

For most people, the decision to buy a home is a very emotional one. And emotional decisions are neither right nor wrong. However, it's important to recognize that buying a house to live in has little to do with its investment potential.

When you are thinking about buying a house, ask yourself the following questions.

WHERE DO I WANT TO LIVE?

Your parents or grandparents may have lived in one house for decades. In part, that may be because the chief breadwinner worked at the same job, in the same town, until it was time to retire. That's just not often true anymore. We have become a much more mobile society. Careers are more portable than ever before; people can work from a beach house in Malibu or a high-rise apartment in Beijing.

Overall, the rental market has greatly expanded in recent years, and the shared economy—think Airbnb—makes it possible for you to be more mobile, at work and at home. You will have much more flexibility to pick up and move to advance your career, or to explore the world, if you are renting than if you are locked into a mortgage. This leads directly to the next question.

HOW LONG DO I PLAN TO LIVE IN THE AREA?

Even if the market increases a bit, buying and then selling a home within a few years is probably not going to work out financially. You won't have time to build equity. Despite your best intentions, you will put pictures on the walls, spend money on furnishings, and fix things that are broken. When you go to sell, you've invested more than just the mortgage payments, and you likely will pay commission to a realtor on top of that. If you are renting, however, you may have a year's lease or you may even be renting month to month. You have much greater flexibility to pick up and move. Moss doesn't grow on a rolling stone!

WHAT DO I WANT FROM MY HOUSE?

This is your wish list—all the things you typically tell your realtor. How many bedrooms do you want? How far do you want to commute to work? Do you want a first-floor master suite, a separate office, space for a man cave? Which of these are deal breakers for you? These wish-list items have to do with money insofar as bigger houses in better locations typically cost more. But the items on your wish list have nothing to do with a home as an investment. In fact, just the opposite may be true. Too big or fancy a home may end up making you house poor.

AM I PREPARED TO MAINTAIN MY HOUSE?

When people sell the house they have lived in for a number of years, they typically look at two numbers—their initial purchase price and the price for which the home sells. Unless you buy at the height of the market and sell at the bottom, that second number is typically bigger, sometimes significantly so. But in between, you have a lot of negative cash flow. If the furnace breaks, you must fix it. If the roof leaks, you must replace it. If you're not handy, you may hire out much of the work. If you do the work yourself, you must buy materials; plus, ask yourself, "What is my time worth?" On the other hand, when you rent and the bathroom faucet leaks, you call the landlord.

DO I VIEW MY HOUSE AS A REFLECTION OF WHO I AM?

Be honest with yourself. Is your house a status symbol to you? Do you want to be able to say to your relatives or colleagues, in effect, "My house is bigger than yours, and my neighborhood is cooler, too"? I once owned a sixty-five-hundred-square foot house that I didn't need, but I wanted it. There were four of us living at home, and we're not large people! Did ego play a role in my decision to buy that house? It might have, but it was very private and we didn't host parties, so I certainly didn't show if off much.

Then again, when I was younger, I would walk through

neighborhoods of homes that I knew I couldn't afford and ask, "Why not me?" For me, being able to purchase a large house in a nice neighborhood or a vacation home in the mountains was tantamount to feeling that I'd arrived. It was a marker that motivated me to work smarter every day.

I don't need others to approve of or be jealous of my home, so it was less about wanting to impress others and more about focusing my personal drive. Remember, you get to decide what's right for you, and if that means buying a big house, go for it! Just consider all your options and buy with eyes wide open, aware of why you are making this decision.

PUT THE MONEY IN A DIFFERENT POCKET

Somewhere on someone else's life assembly line, you may have been taught that owning a home was a smart thing to do, because building equity in a home would be putting money in your own pocket instead of in someone else's pocket—the landlord's, if you rent. And to the extent that a mortgage is a form of forced savings, owning a home might make sense for you.

The rate of savings in this country is abysmally low, but most people are fairly disciplined about paying bills, especially the mortgage. However, imagine your mortgage payment is $2,000 a month. You could put that same $2,000 a month in a coffee can from your early twenties until age sixty-five and accumulate $1 million in savings, despite earning zero interest. You could say you did well accumulating money, but you could not say that the coffee can was a good investment.

Say you buy a house for $500,000. Generally, property values rise about 4 percent over the long haul, even factoring in such downturns as the recession of the mid-2000s. Ten years later, you decide to sell, and you get approximately $740,000, based on 4 percent growth. After you subtract a 5 percent real estate commission of $37,000, and all the other expenses that went with owning a home, how did your home do as an investment? What did it cost you to upgrade the kitchen or replace the roof? What about the real estate and school taxes you paid? How much did you pay in mortgage interest and insurance? These costs add up quickly.

Rate of return isn't the only thing to consider. We've seen that when you invest in a 401(k), for example, you can't touch the money until age fifty-nine and a half without incurring significant penalties. Likewise, when you buy a house, you are building up equity, but that cash may not be accessible until you decide to sell. You may take out a loan against your equity, of course, but that adds to your debt and increases your outgoing cash flow.

Ask yourself what would happen if you didn't buy the house. What if you put your money in another pocket instead? The more aggressive you are as an investor, the more you may be rewarded for finding a better investment than owning a home. Instead of getting a 4 percent return less all those expenses, what if you rented and could invest and earn 7 percent with greater flexibility and liquidity?

Investment return cannot be predicted with certainty, any more than increases in residential home values can be. But if you choose to invest your money, you won't pay real estate taxes, mortgage interest, real estate commissions, or the cost of major repairs. If an employment opportunity arose in a different part of the world, you would have more flexibility to pick up and go.

You may be thinking I am pro-renting. Not at all. I know from experience that bias on this issue leads people to accept, without critical thinking, that buying a home with a mortgage is the smartest path to prosperity. I'm sharing an alternate view. If you consider the opposite case I'm making and then decide to buy a home with a mortgage, you will do so with eyes wide open and more confidence!

So, the next step, after deciding you want a mortgage, is to decide what size and type of mortgage. If you are paying 4 percent interest on your mortgage and are getting a 4 percent rate of return on your savings and investments, then there may be no advantage or disadvantage to paying off your mortgage early.

Let's dig deeper. If you believe your investments may earn more than your 4 percent mortgage interest rate, say 7 percent, then you want to own a mortgage for the largest amount the bank will provide you. It's not in your best interest to take money earning 7 percent in an investment account and pay off 4 percent in mortgage debt. If your investment account is earning 7 percent, then you get to keep the extra 3 percent, after paying the interest, versus taking investment money out to pay down your mortgage balance.

Now let's turn this example around. You are a conservative investor and believe you may only earn 3 percent on your savings and investments. Now it is in your best interest to take money out of an account earning 3 percent and pay down a 4 percent mortgage, if you are comfortable giving up control of your money to the bank. Numbers aside, once you pay extra toward your mortgage, you do not have control of those dollars should life throw you a curveball like unemployment or an illness. Investment accounts at any growth rate are generally very liquid, and you are in control.

Life isn't lived on a spreadsheet. Again, there are no good or bad choices. Many financial choices that seem difficult or involve great uncertainty can be approached in this manner, using critical thinking to determine *what you want your money to do for you.*

Using a mortgage to buy a home may or may not make sense. Likewise, despite what you may have heard about college being a good investment, you might—depending on what you want to do with your life—be throwing your money away. We'll examine more "Financial Planning 101" blasphemy and conventional thinking in the next chapter.

Are you feeling stronger? Are your choices becoming clearer? Or are you more confused than ever? If you are a bit confused, it's okay, because it means you are being made aware of new, unfamiliar, or different points of view that may have you off balance for a bit. It's all good. I have your best interests in mind, so let's move forward together!

COLLEGE: CAREER BOON OR BOONDOGGLE?

You don't need a college degree to be successful in life.

You may want a college degree. You may have been told you should go to college because a college degree may help you be successful in life. You may be telling others that they should go to college, as well. But most people absolutely do not need a college degree to be successful.

If you are studying to be an engineer or a scientist, a college degree and possibly advanced degrees may be required for you to reach your goals. But too many kids go off to college simply because they are on somebody else's life assembly line.

For many, including you, college may be a grotesque waste of money that ends up costing more than dollars and cents. It may result in years of lost opportunity. Your self-esteem may also take a hit as you are pursuing someone else's dream or goal, not yours!

If everyone thinks that *everyone should go to college*, I reflexively begin making the opposite case with critical thinking. Let's take a deeper dive.

DO YOU REALLY NEED THAT DEGREE?

More than thirty years ago, I went to college because I was told that's what I should do to be successful. Neither my parents nor I applied critical thinking to the decision. Believing college was a requirement for success was akin to religion in my family. College was the way and the light, period.

I completed a degree in finance. Along the way, I was forced to take a slew of electives. I took fifteen credit hours in psychology, which I enjoyed. I studied trigonometry, chemistry, physics, history, and English. None of those courses has made me a better entrepreneur. Zero percent of my life's success is attributable to information I received in college classrooms. *Information isn't knowledge, and knowledge certainly isn't wisdom.*

What I benefited from most during my college years was the growing up I did and the experiences I had outside the classroom. But I could have had those same experiences elsewhere without the tuition cost and the heartache of chemistry and geometry. And I still would have been four years older, and hopefully wiser, if I'd done something else with my time.

Times were different and hindsight is 20/20! Nowadays there are so many ways to acquire information and knowledge outside a college classroom. I believe the case against a conventional education gets stronger every month.

I would dare say that more than half of the people who attended college aren't working in the field of their degree, ten-plus years after graduation. If you are, great. If you are not, would you have predicted it at your graduation ceremony? Candidly, I don't know where my diploma is right now. I learn by doing. You may, as well.

EGO AND BIAS REAR THEIR UGLY HEADS

People attend college for various reasons, and some of those reasons may not hold up to the light of critical thinking.

If you do well in high school and are in a certain socioeconomic class, there is a definite bias toward getting a four-year college degree. You should attend college and are expected to get a degree, whether or not you know what you want to study. If you can't afford to pay cash for college, you are encouraged to apply for scholarships and take out loans. The momentum and pressure on many eighteen-year-old children to follow this path is tremendous.

You may attend college because you think that recruiters or hirers will look more favorably on your application if you have a degree in their field. I belong to entrepreneurial groups, and some make the point that a college degree is a red flag. The red flag is that a graduate often believes they know a lot more than they actually know and their attitude is one of entitlement. That is not an attractive combination to entrepreneurs who create and live in a world where results matter and trying does not.

Often, what a college degree says to a prospective employer is that you could finish college, and as I've noted, finishing is an important skill. But there are plenty of people with discipline and work ethic who don't have a college degree. A college degree isn't the goal. The goal is what you will be able to do if you have the college degree versus not having the college degree.

Our old friend "ego" may play a role in decisions about college. For parents, saying, "My daughter goes to Stanford," might sound better than saying, "My daughter is a barista." Are you pushing your children toward college so you have a better story to tell your friends and colleagues? It's a fair question for you to ask yourself or your children.

Finally, you may attend college because you've read studies that say you'll have a higher income than someone who doesn't have a college degree. These studies are flawed because they examine the masses. We are talking about you or your child. If you are intelligent, disciplined, hardworking, and driven to succeed, any potential gap in earnings that results from your not earning a degree is bound to be smaller than the average pay gap of every person who didn't obtain a college degree.

WHERE THE RUBBER MEETS THE ROAD

Considering a four-year college gets very real when you start to run the numbers. Let's compare Sally and Sam.

Sally and Sam are equally talented, but only Sally decides to attend college. Her costs are $30,000 a year for tuition, room, and board. Sam gets a job earning $30,000 a year as an assistant manager at a toy store.

At the end of four years, Sally has paid $120,000, and Sam has earned $120,000. This means Sally is now $240,000 behind where Sam is. That's a lot to catch up on. Sam has likely received raises or a promotion and is now more marketable with four years of work experience. Sam, having worked in the real world, may have a better idea of where he wants to take his career. Sally may have a degree that has high economic value and closes the $240,000 gap quickly. However, Sally's route to financial success comes with much higher financial risk, for sure!

ALTERNATIVE WAYS TO INVEST IN YOUR CHILDREN'S FUTURE

Many parents think about college as an investment in their children's future. But what if there were other ways of doing that? I know I wasn't ready or worthy of the level of investment my parents made in me during my first year of college. Sorry, Mom and Dad.

Maybe you have a child who wants to start a business or backpack through Europe. If this were my child, here's what I might say to them:

> *I'm going to invest in you.* I'm going to give you $30,000 your first year out of high school. You can do with it what you want: start a business, go to Europe and

journal your experiences, go to college—whatever fits in your life plan.

If going to college fits in their life plan, and they can articulate why this helps them achieve their outcomes, then I may be on board. I'm not going to be spending $30,000 because I think I should or to feed my ego. As a parent or child paying for college, you should examine the economics. Including a lifetime of lost interest and opportunity cost, a college education is one of the largest investments you may make in your lifetime, and you are betting on an eighteen-year-old. Think about that for a moment.

RELATIONSHIPS ARE EVERYTHING

My clients initially come to me for my knowledge of financial planning and strategies, but that's not why they keep coming back. When you're in business, *relationships are everything*. How you communicate, how you promote, how you connect with people—that's what matters. Knowledge and technical skill are both very important in my work. But if I were unable to connect with people and build trusting relationships, my knowledge and technical expertise would not matter.

What's really at a premium these days are what I call "soft skills." Politeness, manners, sending thank-you notes, being able to communicate well orally and in writing. Showing up on time, showing up five minutes early, showing initiative. Finishing a project fifteen minutes early and asking others on the staff what you can do to help. As a business owner, I find that those are the attitudes that really stand out in employees, and these skills are not acquired in a book or a college course.

A BRAVE NEW WORLD

Happily, I think the world is beginning to change in ways that support alternatives to expensive, four-year college degrees. There seems to be less stigma attached to attending a community college or a trade school, both of which focus on practical education designed to be applied in a field of employment or trade.

The Internet has opened a whole world of possibilities, not just through random searches but also through online courses, many of them free. You may access most of the information you'd receive during many four-year liberal arts, business, and other nonscientific degree programs. If you know as much as college graduates without even going to college, this doesn't mean the Internet, as a source of your knowledge, receives the same respect from an employer as a college degree. But this is changing, fast!

Results matter, and the world seems to be giving less credit to simply putting in the (four-year) time. I think this is a healthy change, as we have seen young people in their twenties and thirties change the world with technology and entrepreneurial businesses.

More and more people are deciding to become entrepreneurs. Women are in a much better position to create their own future than they were thirty years ago. More small businesses are now created by women than men.

Throughout this discussion and the previous one on buying a home, we've talked about being in debt. You might think I believe that debt is a bad thing. Far from it. Debt is also a financial tool. But there is a big difference between good debt and bad debt, which we'll examine in the next chapter.

ALL DEBT IS NOT CREATED EQUAL

Is it better to have debt or not have debt?

This may seem like an easy question to answer—not having debt is better. Let me ask essentially the same question a different way: Would you prefer to spend your own money or someone else's money? Debt is someone else's money.

There is a difference between good debt and bad debt. Good debt is the outcome of a sober, logical choice made in the best interest of your specific situation. Bad debt is foolishly compromising your future. Yes, we all get to decide what is logical and foolish!

Bad debt is the outcome of reckless spending or living beyond your means and is often fueled by ego. Maybe you buy a house or a car you can't afford, because you want to be seen as the type of person who can own such luxuries. If you get in over your head buying discretionary things that have everything to do with "wants" and nothing to do with "needs," you can end up with a lot of bad debt. Financial concerns often lead to unhappiness, divorces, and other negative outcomes.

Of course, you can also end up with debt because life threw you a curveball or two, in the form of unexpected medical bills, lost employment, or a costly divorce (see the next chapter). In this chapter, we'll examine the concept of good debt and what it can do for you.

WHERE CREDIT IS KING

People in our grandparents' or even our parents' generation may have paid everything with cash. In their minds, this was a virtue. However, it's becoming increasingly difficult not to have a credit card. Try renting a car with cash; it can't be done. You may be able to use a debit card, which links to your bank account, but you are still going to have to carry plastic in your wallet for many everyday conveniences.

In fact, I think cash may effectively disappear altogether within the next ten to fifteen years. Think about it. Whether you're buying jeans, fueling a car, or shopping on Amazon, you likely are using a credit card. Even when you buy a cup of coffee and a muffin, you may use a smartphone app, because it's so much easier than taking physical cash out of your pocket and getting physical change back.

BE WORTHY OF GETTING CREDIT

No one is born with a credit history. Young people are sometimes surprised when they can't get a loan; they think they must be a good credit risk because they don't owe anyone anything. But creditors want to know whether you can handle debt. If you've never been in debt, you have no established credit history.

What's essential for a good credit rating is that you must incur debt and then handle your debt responsibly. Use your credit card often, and pay your credit card balance every month. Pay on time. Don't exceed your credit limit. This is how you show your creditworthiness.

The key takeaway message is that even if you don't like being in debt, you need to prove that you are worthy of being given credit. This is how you build a high credit score, which can be very powerful when you don't have enough money on hand for something you want, or, if the unexpected happens, for something you truly need.

SPEND YOUR MONEY OR SOMEONE ELSE'S MONEY?

Let's examine some alternative scenarios to see how debt may help you secure the outcomes you want in life. Consider Tanya and Tom.

Tanya has no money and owes nothing; she is even with the world. Tom has $500,000 in cash and owes $500,000 to a bank. In effect, he is also even with the world. Tom could, of course, take his cash and pay off his loan, and then he'd be in the same position as Tanya. But Tom has choices that Tanya doesn't have.

Perhaps Tom's loan is the mortgage on his house. He made a choice about his quality of life and purchased a nice home in an up-and-coming neighborhood, with a yard for his children to play in. He had a good credit rating, which allowed him to secure a mortgage at 4 percent interest. Tom's $500,000 mortgage is a good debt for Tom.

Now, let's assume Tom is young and open to a little bit of risk. He doesn't need his $500,000 in cash right away, so he finds an investment that he believes will pay him 7 percent over the long haul. As a financial advisor, I will be the first one to tell you that no one can guarantee the performance of an investment in the future. However, as a practical matter, the anomalies of market crashes and recoveries level out over time.

If Tom's investment performs and he earns 7 percent on his money, he is now 3 percent ahead of where he would have been had he taken the cash and paid down his mortgage. In this case, Tom made the decision that was right for him, and it paid off.

But let's say Tom is a conservative investor. He doesn't want to put his money at risk, so he chooses what he believes to be a low-risk investment paying 3 percent interest. In this case, Tom is losing 1 percent every day that he holds on to an investment paying 3 percent interest while he pays 4 percent interest on his mortgage. However, this might make sense if Tom needs that money in the short term.

Perhaps Tom has a child heading to college in two years. Tom can't afford to tie up his money for the long term, so he chooses the more conservative investment. His short-term financial objective is more important to Tom than the percentage point in interest he is losing.

Likewise, if Tom puts his extra money into paying down

his mortgage, he may not have easy access to the funds when he wants cash for a financial objective. Paying down the mortgage is not the same as opening a checking or savings account with the bank. Tom may or may not be able to borrow against the value of his home if he wants that money back for any reason.

There are tax implications to these decisions that are beyond the scope of this discussion, but they are definitely something you should explore with a trusted tax or financial advisor. However, the bottom line is simple: *you have choices based on what you want your money to do for you.* You can incur debt, and choose to hold it for a period of time, if doing so helps you get what you want out of life. And there is no magic date at which you must pay down your debt, because you will never not owe something to someone.

YOU'LL NEVER PAY EVERYTHING YOU OWE, SO GO HAVE FUN!

Even the richest person in the world will die with bills to pay, and you will be no different.

When you die, there will be final heating bills, phone bills, cable bills, and the like. To the extent that your estate covers your outstanding debts, they will be paid. But if your debts exceed your assets, your lenders have no recourse. Your children are not responsible for paying your debts.

The power company cannot say to your son or daughter, "Your parents lived high on the hog without actually owning enough hog. You need to pay us." Well, they can say whatever they want, but they have no standing to collect.

For many folks in retirement, their primary financial objective may have been to pay off the mortgage on their home. You may recognize yourself in this example. Perhaps you are sitting on a home that's now worth $400,000. You own the contents of the home and maybe a car or two. It's likely that selling the house, the contents, and the cars will more than cover any debt you might have.

Why would you sit on top of all of this wealth and not use some of it for your fun and lifestyle?

Let's say you have always wanted to go to Switzerland and learn how to yodel. What would be the harm if you took a $25,000 loan against your house to fulfill this lifelong dream? The value of your house is still the value of your house. You still own the contents and the cars. But now you've just taken the trip of a lifetime. You used the money for your fun and lifestyle.

The loser, if we must identify one, would be the person who stands to inherit your estate. Rather than $400,000 plus the contents of the house and the cars, they will get $375,000 and all the rest. That's still a nice sum of money, which they can use for their fun and lifestyle.

Never forget that your wealth will either be used for your fun and lifestyle or for someone else's. You cannot take it with you! While many consumers continue to employ the same strategies during retirement that they did while working, I gain great satisfaction in helping clients use their money efficiently in ways that serve their true objectives. There are many tools that exist in our economy. The proper tools in proper hands may be powerful in helping you get the most out of your life!

Debt is a powerful tool and can be destructive. A difficult divorce or business failure can set a person back financially. We'll examine the financial bonuses and pitfalls of marriage in the next chapter.

TILL DEATH DO US PART?

When you marry, you do so with the highest hopes and best intentions.

There is nothing more powerful in life than being in a loving, secure marriage. And marriage has some wonderful financial benefits as well. However, whether you are a starry-eyed young person just starting out, or a mature individual starting over, you need to be clear about the financial choices you are about to make. Decisions made in haste, without all the information you need, may come back to haunt you. In this chapter, we'll examine the financial pluses and minuses of marriage, and how to plan well for a secure future.

ALL FOR ONE AND ONE FOR ALL

In my parents' generation, and even to some extent in mine, individuals pooled their accounts when they married. "What's mine is yours, and what's yours is mine" was often the default position. That's neither good nor bad; it's just what typically was done, especially if only one spouse was working.

Today, however, when two people marry, they may be older, with established careers and separate identities. They may be on a second or third marriage. Often, they have different ways of handling money. If you are in this situation, you are not alone.

But now you face some important decisions, well beyond what to serve the guests at your wedding. Specifically, if you each have your own accounts, do you keep them separate, or do you merge them? Do you create a joint checking and/or savings account? Do you open a credit card in both names? As we have seen throughout this book, there is no right or wrong answer—*there is only the choice that makes sense for you*, and now for your partner, as well.

There may, in fact, be some good reasons to maintain separate accounts. Perhaps you have good credit, but your spouse doesn't. You may want to hang on to your own accounts, at least initially, so you can apply for large purchases with your favorable credit rating. Ideally, this allows your partner time to catch up and repair their credit. But think carefully about what a bad credit score says about your partner's ability to be responsible with their money.

There may also be a great disparity in wealth between you and your future spouse. Is the wealth you accumulated prior to meeting or marrying "the one" to be shared equally? For some, this is a difficult question, and for others, it's easy.

These are the types of thorny issues that lead some couples to consider a prenuptial agreement. A prenuptial agreement is a legal document that outlines issues, often financial, related to potential dissolution of a marriage. Therein lies the difficulty! You are committing your love and devotion to someone for the rest of your natural life, yet drafting an exit strategy if your marriage fails.

This decision is often fraught with emotion, and there is no one-size-fits-all answer. Many of us marry for the first time when we are in our twenties or thirties and haven't accumulated significant wealth. Therefore, the issue is moot. Those of us getting married for a second or third time are generally older and possibly more mature and less emotional about the sometimes-volatile combination of love and money. A trusted legal advisor can help you separate feelings from facts and make the decision that is right for you, as individuals and as a couple. This analytical approach, the prenup, is admittedly not everyone's cup of tea, myself included.

Ultimately, the most important thing you can do is talk about these issues with your partner. Be certain that your expectations are in line with your partner's expectations. If you avoid these decisions, financial disagreements may cause a significant wedge in your relationship—perhaps not when everything is rosy, but definitely if things start to break down.

THE TAX MAN GIVETH, AND THE TAX MAN TAKETH AWAY

The IRS supports marriage. There are huge advantages in the tax code for filing a joint return. Let's consider David and Deborah.

David and Deborah are working, and each makes $50,000 a year. As a single person, each is taxed on their respective income. When they marry and file jointly, they now have $100,000 of combined income to report.

The federal tax burden on $100,000 of total income when David and Deborah file separate returns as single people—reporting $50,000 each—is substantially higher than on the same $100,000 of income when they file their income-tax return as married filing jointly.

Additionally, if David is the only one working, and he makes $100,000 a year, his $100,000 income is taxed significantly less when he marries Deborah.

There are also tax advantages for nonworking spouses. Before they marry, David (employed) can contribute to an IRA because he has earned income, but Deborah (not employed) cannot. When they marry, Deborah, as a non-working spouse, can contribute to an IRA. This is a huge benefit to her, and to the couple's retirement planning, if they decide that having an IRA makes sense for them.

On the flip side of this marital coin, if David and Deborah divorce, they are right back where they started, filing their taxes as individuals, with the "penalties" that come with being a single taxpayer. (The same is true for the surviving spouse if one of them dies.) But there are other costs to divorce as well.

TWO SETS OF EVERYTHING

Being married and working together as a team can be financially efficient. You have one kitchen table, one set of silverware, one set of glasses, one garage, and so forth. But then you get divorced, and one of you moves out. The spouse who leaves must live somewhere, in an apartment or in another home.

Now, there are two kitchen tables, two sets of silverware, two sets of glasses, two garages, and on and on. Expenses go up while tax advantages go away. Divorce is rarely pretty, but even if the divorcing couple gets along perfectly, they still have increased expenses and reduced revenues. And expenses go way up if you have children.

Though our society is changing—in many ways for the better—more often than not, mothers win custody and fathers lose custody. Each state handles child support differently, but in many cases, the cost of raising your children is determined by a judge who likely will never meet your children or give a hoot about your personal values and objectives in raising your children. Alimony and/or child support increase expenses in a mandatory legal ruling. Plus, the legal fees a couple spends to reach an agreement may cost tens of thousands of dollars!

In our example, if David and Deborah get divorced and have two children, it is very likely that Deborah will win custody of the children and David will become the non-custodial parent. Their combined expenses will increase, while their combined income, net of taxes, will decrease. This is not a good financial combination.

The divorce process and child-support determination are very much lived on a spreadsheet, with numbers driven by the judge. The parent with custody, Deborah in our example, has outsized influence, compared to David, on the children's upbringing, discipline, values, and even when David may see the children. If David is paying Deborah child support, Deborah also has great latitude on how that money is spent, while David has none.

Children of a divorced couple see the custodial parent, typically the mother, buy them things and save for their college education, without having any idea that much of this money comes from the noncustodial parent, usually the father. This may be especially true when the children are young.

In our example, if David pays for his children's clothes, food, or school supplies directly, that money is in addition to his child-support payments. David is, in effect, paying twice to help support his children.

With David working overtime, often literally, to help support his children as the noncustodial parent, his career performance may suffer, and that further imperils his wallet. It's difficult to perform your best when you are frustrated, feeling helpless, or missing your children. This isn't surprising to read, I'm sure, but these aspects of divorce and their cumulative financial impact often are not anticipated.

These outcomes are the same if you switch David's and Deborah's names in my example. Regardless, the financial impact is huge. There are many reasons for getting a divorce, and divorce may be the absolute best decision for you and your family, but I want you to recognize the financial cost of divorce and act with your eyes wide open.

WHEN DEATH DO US PART

In a traditional wedding ceremony, we pledge to stay together for better or for worse, in sickness and in health, till death do us part. Since death is a fact of life, and one spouse typically dies before the other, the grieving widow or widower is left to pick up the pieces.

When your spouse dies, you will experience all sorts of emotions, regardless of how strong your relationship was. In any marriage, especially over time, you tend to parcel off who does what, and now all of the sudden, at a very difficult time, one of you has to do what the other one did.

Maybe you've never done a load of laundry or cooked a meal in your life. Or maybe your spouse handled the finances, and you have no idea where all the accounts are and how to access them. You don't know how you will pay your bills or even where to pick up your dry cleaning or prescription medication.

Added to that, you will now face the same higher income taxes for being widowed as you would if you'd gotten divorced. This confusion creates fear at a time when you may be overwhelmed with grief. This is not a good position to be in.

Again, being transparent and talking about these issues well in advance can save a lot of problems when the time comes. Addressing these issues is simple but not at all easy. We get busy, and there are plenty of other things to do and discuss. But there are actions you may take in advance.

First, create an overall checklist or inventory of all your accounts. Because much of our financial business is transacted online, write down your passwords and let your partner know where they are. It's better to keep all this information electronically, because paper is more easily lost, burned, or discarded. Just be certain that your partner and any others who will need this information know how to access it.

Second, don't delay making out a will or setting up a trust (see more about this in chapter 17). Do your due diligence in finding an attorney with whom you feel comfortable. I know that no one likes to think about dying, but you must do this before you become incapable of doing so—or, worse, before you die without specifying your wishes. Be certain that your beneficiary designations are up to date. You may always change these documents as your life circumstances change, provided you are not incapacitated.

Third, plan for how you would deal with loss of income. Often, when you lose a spouse, one or both of you are retired. The surviving spouse will collect less Social Security than when you were both alive. If one of you has a traditional pension, the benefit to the survivor will likely be reduced.

I know much of what is covered in this chapter may be difficult to contemplate. We don't think about divorce or death when we marry. But despite our best intentions, life can throw us a curveball or two, and it helps to be prepared. Read the next chapter to discover how we can learn from the past without carrying it with us.

THE GODFATHER AND DECISION MAKING IN TIMES OF INTENSITY

There is a scene in *The Godfather* that crystallizes my attitude toward life.

Right after Rocco Lampone kills Paulie Gatto in a parked car, mobster Peter Clemenza orders Lampone to "leave the gun." But he remembers the baked goods he promised his wife, so he adds, "Take the cannoli." Yes, I love *The Godfather* movies and want to make a connection. Here it is.

We all experience conflict in our life, big and small. Strive to "leave the gun," and let go of the bad. You may choose to leave behind all your bad decisions—financial and otherwise—that you have ever made, and move past all the difficult things that have ever happened to you. This is not an easy choice, but recognize that it is a choice—a choice only you have the power to make.

You may also choose to "take the cannoli," to never forget the sweet things in life, the good things that happen each and every day to all of us. You choose how you act, what you think about, and how you treat others.

I'm not saying you want to put three bullets in the back of someone's head for any reason. I am saying that the past is the past, and you can't change a minute of it. Certainly, the past can be instructive, but if you're carrying around mistakes and disappointments like so much heavy baggage, set it down. Walk around it. Let it go. It's okay to rent your past, but *you don't have to own it*. Accept responsibility, but choose to own your future actions!

My goal throughout this book is to help you make better life decisions and, therefore, better financial decisions. In this chapter, I'll share with you some of the life experiences that have shaped my thinking and steeled my decision-making skills. You may be better equipped to avoid life's potholes than I was.

BORN AGAIN, OR HITTING THE RESET BUTTON

I know firsthand how painful failure can be, but also how much good can come from those failures.

When my first marriage failed and I got divorced, I had two beautiful young daughters. I naïvely thought I could leave a destructive relationship with my girls' mother, while not impacting my close relationship with our two girls.

My failure in my first marriage also remains one of the most confusing life scenarios I've ever encountered. How can anyone date, get married, have children, and spend most of their daily life together with someone—for six years in my case—and yet harbor so much hate? I didn't understand the hatred then or now. However, my cluelessness had a financial impact and provided valuable lessons for me.

As an entrepreneur, I am compensated based on performance, and my performance was declining. My life was chaotic, and my finances suffered. I learned that I don't get to choose what someone else does or thinks. If my ex-spouse wanted to spend her time hating me, I had to put on my big-boy pants and work within that reality.

I didn't understand the hatred, but after about five years, I finally recognized that I was feeding the hatred with my frustration. Attempts to have a rational discussion with my daughters' mother about handling school or discipline, requesting more time with my daughters, or addressing financial concerns were stoking the hatred. Why would anyone, let alone the mother of my daughters, want to make my life more difficult simply for the enjoyment?

I'm sure some of you reading this are chuckling about now. Clearly, I was clueless and naïve. If you have children and are considering divorce, or when you have challenging days in your marriage, know that everything about divorce is much more difficult than you can possibly imagine. This doesn't mean you shouldn't get divorced; it simply means you cannot know how difficult that experience is likely to be.

I became a born-again Christian about this time, which may mean a lot of different things to different people. To me, that experience was as important and impactful as any event to that point in my life. This isn't a book on faith, but my faith has guided my life and financial decisions ever since.

My faith led me to tell my ex-spouse that I was sorry for anything I had ever done to disappoint her and that I forgave her for anything she ever did to me. The weight of the world seemed to be lifted from my shoulders. I no longer sought to win an argument. I recognized it didn't matter if I was correct unless there was a better outcome for my daughters. I refused to fight. I also forgave myself for all that I had contributed to a failed marriage.

This is personal, and my experiences may not be your experiences. However, divorce has led many couples to financial ruin. The mental tax may also last for many years. Seeking the strength inside you through faith or the *flowers in your garden*, you can learn from the past without remaining stuck there. This will likely lead you to new heights of accomplishment.

"STRONG AT THE BROKEN PLACES"

You know that old saying, "What doesn't kill you makes you stronger"? Ernest Hemingway had a wonderful way of expressing this. He wrote, "The world breaks everyone, and afterward, some are strong at the broken places."

When you are chugging along on the life assembly line, you rarely get time to stop and reflect. You pay the bills, you play with the children, you climb the career ladder. I was doing all of that, and more.

When my world came crashing down, I had to take a good hard look at myself and the way I'd been living my life. I became, in Hemingway's words, "strong at the broken places"—not in spite of what I went through, *but because of it.*

I had to help raise two young girls, navigate a poisonous relationship with their mother, nurture a new marriage that included stepchildren, and run my businesses. I couldn't sit at the stoplight and think. I had to either go left or go right. I had to keep moving, and this honed my innate ability to be a creative problem solver. You may have also discovered that you were stronger than you thought when your chips were down.

I became more decisive and began to view my failures as tuition in the school of hard knocks, rather than beating myself up for my mistakes. I stopped looking backward and began looking only forward. Perhaps for this reason, I don't go to high school reunions and I'm not a fan of photo albums. If you are, more power to you!

I learned that forgiveness is not for the other person; it's for you. Letting go of the past—of the pain, anger, and regrets—was transformational for me.

I would not be where I am today—emotionally, financially, or career-wise—if I hadn't been tested with fire. Don't get me wrong; I'm not suggesting that anyone go through this as an intentional path to success!

I coined the phrase "sit fat" in my family. It was 1998 in the Wrigley Field bleachers, while watching a Chicago Cubs game with my brothers, their wives, and my wife, Dawn.

The phrase "sit fat" means "hold your tongue." Even if I know I'm correct on a point of fact, I no longer feel I must "win" every argument or prove it. When you're in a discussion that begins to get heated, you can simply stop, agree to disagree, or walk away. In far more cases than you realize, "winning" an argument is losing. This is especially true in marriages and other close relationships. Try it! Sit fat next time you want to pounce with the perfect comeback line.

AN ATTITUDE OF GRATITUDE

We often take life, or ourselves, too seriously. None of us is indispensable. We need to give ourselves permission to take a "snow day."

When I grew up in Iowa and Illinois, there were days when my siblings and I went to bed expecting to go to school the next day. Waking up to bad weather, we would turn on the radio, waiting for the announcer to go alphabetically through all the schools. When we heard our school was closed for the day, it was just awesome!

As an adult and an entrepreneur, every great once in a

while I will get to the office, turn on my computer, and realize that I'm just not feeling it, so I'll head home for a "snow day." I might be tired of too many "shoulds" or simply need to recharge. I've grown better at forgiving myself, and I come back the next day stronger.

I've learned to check my ego at the door and do my best not to let my biases color my opinions. Certainly, I had plenty of reasons to have a negative view of marriage, but I don't blame the concept of marriage because my first one failed. That was on me. I was young, immature, and too focused on getting down the life assembly line.

In my financial planning practice, I help prospective clients separate past negative experiences with financial products and strategies from what is in their best interests now. A strategy or product might have been poorly applied in the past. A failure or negative experience is likely not due to the product or strategy, but to poor advice or application.

Finally, I've learned that we all make decisions we come to regret, financial and otherwise. Our challenge is to *learn from them and move on*. Critical thinking may help you avoid many of life's pitfalls and lead to better decision making. In the next chapter, we'll examine how critical thinking applies to investing.

DON'T BE AN EASY MARK WHEN YOU INVEST

P. T. Barnum is credited with saying, "There's a sucker born every minute," and an important aspect of my work as a financial planner is to make sure that sucker isn't you.

You need to make decisions with your eyes wide open. This is true in life, and it is certainly true when it comes to investing your hard-earned money. Whether you are a "do-it-yourselfer" or you hire a professional, it helps if you understand how things work.

LOOK AT BOTH SIDES NOW

In the days before compact discs and streaming music,

there was vinyl. Music was recorded on both sides of an album, though typically one side had the better cuts, so you may not have played the flip side as often. In investing, however, it helps to be aware of what's on both sides of any financial transaction or decision.

Let's say you are comfortable doing your own investing, and you want to buy stock in the ABC Company because they make your favorite running shoe. You can walk into an ABC store and buy the running shoes, but you can't purchase shares of ABC stock in the same way.

To simplify the example, let's imagine that all shares of ABC stock are owned by a single investor. We'll call him Joe. Joe is holding on to his ABC stock, which is currently valued at $109 a share.

You want to buy ABC stock, and you're willing to pay $111 a share, but Joe isn't willing to sell at that price, because he believes the share price will go higher. You really want to own stock in the ABC Company, so you decide you're willing to pay $115 a share. Now Joe is willing to sell.

Let's look at both sides of this transaction.

You want to buy ABC stock at $115 a share because you anticipate the price of the stock will rise, maybe to $125 a share and beyond. You think you're getting a good deal because you feel optimistic about the future of the company.

Joe is willing to sell because he doesn't think the price will go any higher than $115 per share. If he did, he would likely hold on to his stock. Joe thinks he's getting a good deal because he believes the company is overvalued and the share price can only decline from $115.

This type of transaction takes place millions of times a day. Whether you are buying individual stocks or shares of a mutual fund, there are only so many outstanding shares available. Every time you buy shares because you believe the value will increase, you likely do not realize that the person selling the shares to you is equally certain the value will decline from the price you are paying.

DON'T BUY INTO THE COMPANY JUST BECAUSE YOU LIKE THE COFFEE

When you buy stocks, you are choosing to be part owner of a company. Perhaps it's a very tiny part, but that's what stock represents. It represents ownership.

Many people want to own stock in companies whose products they love. In fact, stocks in such companies as Apple and Tesla have a sort of cult following. Perhaps a bit of ego is involved. When you're at a cocktail party and the discussion turns to investing, you may want to show that you own some "sexy" stocks.

But just because you fall in love with a company's products doesn't mean you must own the company as a stockholder. That's a completely different decision.

Let's say you are interested in the local coffee shop on the corner. You love their coffee. You love their service. You have a positive experience every time you stop in.

But if you want to own a piece of the company, you must examine the books. Maybe this company is losing money because they're putting super premium ingredients in that awesome cup of coffee and they're paying their baristas well to be so attentive. When you lift the hood as a potential investor, you say, "Whoa! I'll drink their delicious coffee, but this business model can't last unless something changes."

WOULD YOU LOAN A BANK MONEY?

When you buy stocks, you own part of a company. In contrast, when you buy a corporate bond, you are loaning a company money.

Jill banks with XYZ Bank down the street from her house.

She could buy XYZ stock, but the company also issues bonds, which pay interest. Jill decides to purchase a $10,000 bond paying 3 percent interest for ten years. She is exchanging $10,000 of her cash for this promissory note called a bond.

Again, let's look at both sides of this transaction.

Jill agrees to give XYZ Bank the use of her $10,000 and expects to earn 3 percent or $300 every year for ten years. She thinks she's getting a good deal because she feels her money is in a low-risk investment.

XYZ Bank agrees to issue a bond to Jill paying 3 percent over ten years. They feel they are getting a good deal because they believe they can make much more than 3 percent while they have use of Jill's money. That doesn't mean the investment is wrong for Jill, but she needs to be aware that there are two sides to every transaction.

Now, let's imagine Jill wants to earn more than 3 percent on her $10,000. The ABC Bank is paying 6 percent on its bonds, so Jill thinks that's a much better deal. But is it?

Let's hold this up to the light and apply critical thinking.

If the ABC Bank could borrow money at 3 percent rather

than 6 percent, why wouldn't it do so? The most likely reason the ABC Bank is paying a higher interest rate is because it can't sell its bonds (borrow) without paying 6 percent interest. Maybe ABC Bank is not as well established as XYZ Bank. Maybe ABC Bank has a limited track record in the industry. For the investor, a 6 percent bond from ABC Bank carries more risk than a 3 percent bond from XYZ Bank.

This is not unlike what happens when two people go to the bank to get a mortgage. The one with a better credit score will get a loan at a more favorable interest rate. The one with the worse credit—the riskier buyer, as far as the bank is concerned—will pay a higher interest rate.

The same principle is at work in our example of two banks paying vastly different rates on their bonds. You must know the creditworthiness of the company whose bonds you want to buy, because if the ABC Bank can't make interest payments or goes under, the bond won't be worth the paper it's printed on. If you are open to this level of risk, ABC bonds may be for you. If not, you might choose a less risky bond like the XYZ bond with the lower interest rate.

A LITTLE GOES A LONG WAY

Some people feel confident about investing in individual

stocks, while others, like Jill, are more comfortable purchasing bonds. The most common way that individuals invest is in mutual funds. For example, 401(k) plans are dominated by mutual funds on their investment menu.

A stock mutual fund or an exchange-traded fund (ETF) is essentially a basket of stocks. As an example, a mutual fund might own eighty different stocks, of which ABC Bank is one, along with such companies as Apple, Tesla, and Google.

If you own shares of ABC Bank stock and the share price tanks, you may lose a lot of money. However, if you own a mutual fund with ABC stock in it, other stocks may be having a great year, so, overall, you may make money despite ABC Bank stock losses. This example defines diversification, where you don't have all your eggs in one (ABC stock) basket!

There are more than ten thousand mutual funds and ETFs in the United States and more than eighty thousand in the world. Each fund has a financial objective and a minimum investment threshold. Even if you are only able to invest a few hundred dollars, you may effectively become part owner in many different companies by owning a mutual or exchange-traded fund.

You also may be able to diversify with a small initial investment, say $100. Rather than putting all your money into stocks, you may buy a "blended" mutual fund, one in which the fund owns a basket containing a variety of bonds, domestic stocks, international stocks, commodities, and other types of investments.

It's still a mutual fund with a specific share price and minimum investment. But the mutual fund holds a variety of different financial instruments, so now your $100 gets you instant diversification, something you can't do with a small amount of money any other way.

Depending on your level of comfort with investment risk, you can do everything we've talked about in this chapter on your own. Buy stocks. Buy bonds. Buy mutual funds.

You can also change the oil in your car, but maybe you'd rather find a mechanic.

Financial advisors may be mechanics for your money. They may assist you in planning for your fun and lifestyle during retirement. But just as not all mechanics are alike, not all financial professionals are created equal. Read the next chapter to learn how to choose an advisor who is right for you.

IN LIFE, YOU GET WHAT YOU PAY FOR

American oil-well firefighter Red Adair is credited with saying, "If you think it's expensive to hire a professional to do the job, wait until you hire an amateur."

There are many people who insist that it is less expensive to do any task or work yourself. This is small thinking, without any regard for the value of your time and the expertise of others. In most cases, for this to hold true, you must place a low dollar value on your time (likely far below your employment earnings) and believe you are the best person for the job.

Perhaps you're a do-it-yourself investor (DIYI). There

are DIYIs who simply enjoy learning about investing and want to maintain control, and there are DIYIs who think they are more effective at investing than a professional. DIYIs sometimes criticize professionals, yet do not apply critical thinking. Think about this. You and a financial professional know more collectively than you do alone. The financial professional may add to your knowledge and decision making beyond your own understanding. The tricky part is that you don't know if the value you would receive from the professional is worth paying for, and you must pay to find out.

As you would in working with other professionals, you must experience the value and the outcome yourself. I've spent more than half of my life as a financial professional, and I recognize that there is a very wide gap in knowledge between a competent, experienced financial professional and a DIYI or typical consumer. However, there is also a significant experience gap between financial professionals, even if they have the same licenses and qualifications. This is also true with attorneys, physicians, accountants, and other professionals.

DIYIs don't ask themselves challenging questions or pointed follow-up questions. Why would they? DIYIs rarely hold their performance accountable to a standard, probably because the standard would be a professional.

In my experience, this behavior is often due to negative bias that the DIYI has toward financial professionals.

For example, they may have previously hired a professional who wasn't much more than a product salesperson. As a result, the DIYI assumed that all financial professionals were similar and concluded, "I can do as well as they can." Another example of bias is the DIYI's belief that they are saving money. However, the DIYI amateur is often more expensive than the professional.

In most industries, there are retail costs and wholesale costs. Which pricing do you prefer? The mutual fund industry is no different. Most mutual funds in the marketplace have both "retail" share classes and an "institutional" share class.

Let's look at the imaginary DMP mutual fund. The DMP fund has "A" class shares, "B" class shares, "C" class shares, "K" class shares, "Y" class shares, and "I" class shares. Regardless of the specific share class, the DMP fund contains the exact same stocks and other investments. For example, the "share class A" DMP fund is invested exactly the same as the "share class B" DMP fund, so the *gross* (before expenses) rate of return is exactly the same with all share classes. This is very important for you to understand before moving forward.

Let's say the DMP mutual fund has a *gross* rate of return equaling 10 percent. Every share class has this same 10 percent *gross* rate of return. The difference between these share classes is how much of your money goes to pay internal expenses before you receive your *net* rate of return!

So, if a retail share class of DMP, which can be purchased by an amateur or DIYI, has internal expenses of 1.5 percent, the *net* rate of return would be 10 percent minus 1.5 percent, or 8.5 percent. If a professional has access to the institutional share class of DMP, which may have internal expenses of 0.4 percent, the *net* rate of return for the professional using the DMP fund would be 10 percent minus 0.4 percent, or 9.6 percent.

With every mutual fund that has retail share classes and an institutional (wholesale) share class, you will see a significant difference in expenses favoring the institutional share class, which the DIYI may not access. Working with some professionals gives you access to wholesale pricing, which may mitigate or offset the financial professional's fee.

LET'S BE PERFECTLY CLEAR

By now, I hope you've begun to understand that the key to being a savvy investor is understanding what you are paying for—not just what you see on the bottom line of your statement, but everything that goes into it. *Transparency is the name of the game.*

Ostensibly, that's why you receive a prospectus—that thick booklet that shows up in your mailbox or email inbox. By law, if you buy an investment, whether on your own or through an advisor, you'll automatically receive a prospectus. In effect, it's like an owner's manual for the investment security that you bought.

But unlike the owner's manual for your car, which you will likely put in the glove compartment and may refer to from time to time, you may never open the prospectus for your investments. You may even feel conflicted about whether to save it. It looks important, but you have no idea what's in it. And you are not alone. Few people read or understand these documents.

The industry can accurately say you were given everything you needed to know to purchase that security. All the information you need is in the prospectus.

But, as I'm fond of saying, *information isn't knowledge, and knowledge certainly isn't wisdom.* You received a lot of information, but you are no wiser about how your investments really work.

Sadly, there is an appalling lack of financial education in our society, and transparency, even when provided in my industry, is often not absorbed in any meaningful way. For example, a lot of the fees and expenses associated with investments are built inside of the products themselves.

In our earlier example, when you receive an 8.5 percent net rate of return after expenses on your DMP retail share class mutual fund, that's what will show on your statement. You may feel pretty good about that. You may not know—unless you are well informed by an advisor or you do a lot of research that most people don't or won't do—that the fund actually earned a gross rate of return equaling 10 percent. The 1.5 percent in expenses was pulled out of the 10 percent to pay the mutual fund company's business costs, the broker who sold you the mutual fund, and possibly for the blimp and other advertising you see on TV during the golf tournament or the football game.

Really, you have two choices, much as you would with changing the oil in your car. You can peer under the hood and do the dirty work, or you can hire someone to do it. What is your time worth? And where is your expertise? It's the same with financial planning. You can either open the hood on these products and services, or you can hire a pro to do it. My professional colleagues and I pay attention to the fine print, so you can use your time and your money for your fun and lifestyle.

You don't know what you don't know. This statement is true as you read these words and will remain true forever. Professionals—financial and otherwise—have dedicated their talents and their lives to learning their profession and to applying strategies in real-world situations with their clients. My knowledge grows continuously because I participate directly in so many life decisions that my clients ponder and make every week. This creates experience and wisdom that simply cannot be replicated by an amateur.

NOT ALL ADVISORS ARE CREATED EQUAL

My experience tells me that at least half of the people who hire a financial advisor have little idea how that advisor is paid. It's rare in your life that you make a purchasing decision without knowing the prices for the services. I'm happy to shine some light on advisor compensation.

Basically, there are two types of financial professionals you can hire to assist you with investments: a broker or a fee-based advisor. A fee-based advisor is a fiduciary. "Fiduciary" is a fancy legal term for one who does what's in the best interest of the client.

Let's take brokers first. Brokers represent the company for which they work and are paid commission. Their revenue is primarily transaction driven. Every time they buy or sell a mutual fund or individual stock, they may receive a financial reward in the form of a commission.

This is no different than if you were buying a car at the Toyota dealership. The salesperson is representing the Toyota dealership, not you as the consumer, and their objective is to sell Toyotas. Period. There is nothing wrong with that, but that is clearly their objective.

When you are talking to a broker who works for a specific firm, you may think the broker is acting in your best interest, and they may feel they are doing so, too. But from a regulatory and compensation standpoint, the broker is representing their company in the same way the Toyota salesman is representing the Toyota dealership. The broker may want to sell you their mutual fund or annuity, regardless of whether it is in your best interests and fits your lifestyle or needs.

In contrast, a fiduciary, or fee-based advisor, represents the client, not any particular company. There is no conflict of interest, because a fiduciary doesn't receive commission for selling a specific product or service. A fee-based advisor gets paid in one of two ways.

First, you may pay a fee-based advisor (fiduciary) on an hourly basis. You pay for their time and expertise, and then you are free to act or not act on the fiduciary's advice. It's that simple.

Second, you may pay a fee-based advisor to proactively manage your money, and it would typically work like this. At the end of each calendar quarter, the dollar value of your accounts is multiplied by an agreed-upon percentage. Let's say the fiduciary charges a 1 percent fee annually. At the end of each calendar quarter, the dollar value of your accounts multiplied by one-fourth of 1 percent is the quarterly fee paid to the fee-based advisor and typically deducted from your account.

Because you are paying your financial professional based on the value of your accounts rather than for transactions, this means that *you and the fee-based advisor want the exact same outcome*. You want your account to go up in value so you have more money for your fun and lifestyle, and the fee-based advisor also wants the value of your account to go up so their fee percentage is applied to a bigger pile of money.

There are no transactional revenues or commission compensation involved in having a fiduciary manage your investments. The fee-based advisor doesn't get paid for buying or selling stocks, mutual funds, or other investments you hold. The only changes the fee-based advisor makes to your portfolio are based on what is in your best interests. Whether a fee-based advisor makes ten trades for you in a year or one hundred, there isn't one penny of commission associated with those trades.

Let's go back to our example of DMP mutual fund with 1.5 percent in fees inside the retail share class funds versus 0.4 percent in fees within the institutional share class funds. A fiduciary paid to represent you, not a company, would recommend the institutional share class fund that has lower expenses, all else being equal. More money in your account is a win-win for you and for your fee-based advisor. A commission-based broker has a financial stake in transactions, but not the same financial stake in your investment performance.

Additionally, a fee-based advisor financially benefits if you maintain a long-term relationship, because the fee agreement that you and the fiduciary sign lasts only as long as you are working together. Either party may cancel at any time. This creates a natural accountability between the fiduciary and the client. If the client is dissatisfied for any reason, they may fire their fee-based advisor. You may wonder, "Why would the fiduciary ever cancel an agreement that pays them?" The answer is simple—for the same reason that you may prefer not to work with someone. The fee-based advisor may become dissatisfied with the client. Working with a fiduciary is like a trusted partnership, while working with a commission-based broker is closer to working with a product vendor.

CHANGE FOR THE BETTER

I'm pleased to say that over the past decade, the financial services industry is moving toward a fee-based model and away from commission-based sales. There is always an upside and a downside to most regulations, but, on balance, I think a move toward greater transparency in the financial services industry benefits all.

Too often, important questions go unanswered. Remember our old friend ego? You may not want to appear uninformed, so you don't ask the broker to explain terms or concepts you don't understand. Brokers have little incentive to tell you more than they think you need to know to buy a product. There are many well-intentioned, principled financial professionals working as commission-based brokers. However, knowing how your financial professional is compensated will always be relevant.

IT'S NOT WHAT YOU MAKE—IT'S WHAT YOU KEEP!

Ultimately, good financial advisors help you apply critical thinking to the full range of money decisions you must make.

As we've seen throughout this book, many of the decisions you make about how to save and invest your money have significant tax implications. Financial advisors may not have an accounting background or understand how the tax code affects your investing bottom line.

Your financial advisor should pose questions that will guide you in making the decisions that are right for you. We've highlighted two of these questions previously:

- Do I want to pay taxes on the seeds, the money I put into my accounts, or on the harvest, the money I earn in those accounts over many years?
- If I think taxes will be higher in the future, do I want to pay lower taxes now or wait and pay taxes when the rates are higher?

There are no right or wrong answers to these questions. There are only the answers that will help you choose the products and strategies that are right for you.

To help determine the best strategy for you, your financial advisor may use information about your projected retirement income, including Social Security and other retirement accounts, current and planned investments, and previous tax returns, to help you approximate what your future tax bracket will be. This will help you determine the true rate of return on your savings and investments, which is the gross return minus expenses and taxes (called net rate of return).

Remember, *life isn't lived on a spreadsheet.* Even the best financial advisors don't have a crystal ball, so no one can predict how long you will live or what interest or tax rates there will be in the future. But when you share what you want your money to do for you—your money's purpose—a financial advisor may help you make decisions that will support your objectives, values, and lifestyle. Your financial advisor may also guide you in making the decisions that will support your heirs' fun and lifestyle, as the next chapter highlights.

NO ONE GETS OUT ALIVE

If you have the money to do everything in life you want to do, and you can leave the absolute maximum to others after you're gone, that's financial perfection.

I often find myself thinking about the title of the first biography of Jim Morrison, lead singer and lyricist of The Doors, written by Jerry Hopkins nearly a decade after Morrison's death in 1971. The book was called, *No One Here Gets Out Alive*. We don't like to think about it, but death is a part of life. You can't take your money and your stuff with you; however, you may control your money and your stuff from beyond the grave if you make planning decisions while you are able to do so.

REMEMBER, IT'S YOUR MONEY AND YOUR STUFF

Why should you plan for what happens to your money when you're gone? It's simple—if you don't make these decisions, someone else will. In effect, the absence of a decision is a decision.

State laws differ, but if you don't spell out your wishes in a will or by establishing a trust, the court system and a judge you'll never meet are going to follow a set of protocols that are inflexible. Here is an example if you're married with children: in some states, if you die—absent specific legal instructions—any accounts in your name would be split fifty-fifty between your spouse and your children. The default would not be a complete transfer of ownership to your spouse, even if that had been what you wanted.

I know legal documents and decisions may seem intimidating. But keep in mind that *it's your money and your stuff.* Just as you get to decide what to do with your money while you're alive, you get to decide what happens to your money and your stuff after you're gone. You can put whatever you want (provided it's legal) in a legal document, and your wishes will be carried out.

Maybe you've lost touch with your best friend, but you want her to have the stamp collection you worked on together when you were kids. Perhaps you're an animal lover who wants the bulk of your estate to go to the local humane society. It's an attorney's job to put your desires and values in a legal document. It's not their job to tell you what to do with your money and your stuff. Like with all decisions in life, there are benefits and limitations that you may explore prior to crafting these legal documents, which represent you when you are no longer alive.

When I coach people through this process, I can see them begin to relax. Let the attorney worry about the legalese while you focus on what to do with the money and the stuff you accumulated over a lifetime.

DELICATE DECISIONS THAT DON'T INVOLVE MONEY OR STUFF

Estate planning isn't just about what to do with your grandmother's silver tea service. If you have minor children, you'll want to think about who will care for them until they are able to be on their own. When you make a first choice, be sure to communicate it to the person or couple to be certain that they are willing and able to accept this responsibility. It's fair for someone to decline if they don't feel they are up to the task.

Even if you have a willing first choice to be your children's guardian, have a second and a third choice as backups. Planning for contingencies just makes sense. You can update these legal documents as your life circumstances change—for example, if you divorce and remarry, or if you decide to leave the stamp collection to Uncle Harry.

Whom will you choose to administer your will or trust? With a will, you choose an executor, and with a trust, you choose a trustee. The executor or trustee is tasked with carrying out the wishes you have legally established in your will and trusts. If you have three children, you may choose as executor or trustee the oldest child or the one you believe to be more mature or financially savvy at the time you draft the document. This may change over time, so you'll want to review these documents and keep them up to date.

Also, be aware that if you don't discuss your choices with your three children, you may unintentionally offend a child not selected to administer your will or trust. The difficult reality is that when these documents matter, you won't be around to clear up any misunderstandings or soothe hurt feelings.

These are delicate decisions, but they are ones you'll want to make yourself rather than having someone else make them for you. Remember, the absence of a decision is a decision.

IT'S ALL LIFE INSURANCE IN THE END

When you die, everything is basically life insurance. Other than the sentimental mementos, such as your junior high school report card and the pencil holder your son made from a soda can, most everything has a monetary value. Your house will typically be sold and converted to cash. Your car and any stuff the children or grandchildren don't want will be sold off or donated as a tax deduction. Your investments will be dispersed per your wishes (a good reason to keep the designation of your beneficiaries up to date). Without making this too complicated, everything is converted to cash, similar to life insurance policy benefits.

PUT THE PIECES TOGETHER

Always remember, money is just ink on paper. It has no value until you exchange it for something you want. Therefore, *good financial planning is all about you.* In the final chapter, we'll revisit some of the key themes we've highlighted throughout this book and underscore the importance of finding your path to living life to its fullest.

YOU DON'T HAVE TO GO IT ALONE

Life isn't lived on a spreadsheet, and I don't have all the answers you want—but I and other professional advisors have excellent questions that may help you find your answers.

I'm in the business of helping people make better decisions, and most decisions involve money in some way. *I'm in the business of building quality, long-term relationships.* I'm also in the business of intentionally asking questions and listening intently to your answers to learn what you want your money to do for you. Not what Uncle Charles or Cousin Susie thinks you should do, and not what a nameless, faceless Internet site suggests you should do.

Having someone in your corner—someone whose mission and responsibility it is to look out for what's best for you—can be a source of emotional health and financial wealth.

If you've ever played an instrument, then imagine the gap between your skill level and that of a true professional. A guitar or piano sounds very different played by your fingers versus a professional's fingers. Same instruments, dramatically different outcomes.

Growing up, did you you dribble a basketball or bat a baseball? The same basketball or bat in the hands of a true professional seems capable of so much more than what you can accomplish alone.

A writing pen can be used to note your to-do list or, in the hands of a genius, to compose a brilliant song or novel.

You may buy financial products and believe those products will provide the same outcome as a professional advisor may provide. However, if you recognize the difference between an amateur and a professional in all other areas of life, then why would financial planning be different? Fair question? Buying products is not financial planning.

Financial planning is about integration, efficiency, coordination, creativity, and so much more, as the following example attempts to illustrate.

AVOID DECORATING BY COMMITTEE

A comprehensive financial planner seeks to connect seemingly disparate pieces of information so their client receives the best possible outcomes given their circumstances. Financial decisions are by their very nature life decisions, and life decisions can be difficult to make in isolation.

Let's imagine you've decided to redecorate your living room. To help you, I'm going to write you a blank check to cover all expenses associated with this project. Money is no object! There is a catch, however.

I'm actually going to give you five blank checks, because you must choose five friends to go shopping for you. Each of these friends must shop independently of the other four friends, with no communication permitted among them.

Give the first blank check to one of your friends to get the best furniture for your new living room—again, money is no object.

Give the next blank check to the second friend and ask

them to get the best artwork and wall coverings. They can go wherever they want and choose whatever they like.

Give the third blank check to your next friend and have them purchase floor coverings—from Turkish rugs to Italian marble, the sky's the limit.

Give the next blank check to your fourth friend to buy all your electronics—television, stereo, surround sound, the works.

And, finally, give your last friend the final blank check to purchase the finishing touches—window treatments, vases, flowers, potpourri, and so on.

These five friends will come together and install everything in your living room while you're not home. Remember, there was no communication among these friends while shopping. Now you come home to view your redecorated living room for the first time. What does it look like?

If it looks coordinated, it would be random luck. More likely, your living room—decorated by five trusted friends with unlimited budgets—would be a total hodgepodge. Few things would match, and you might have to return everything and start over. But how can this be? They bought the best of everything!

If you are like many people I see, you may approach financial planning the same way. You may have the best investment broker on the planet to help you invest your hard-earned cash. Separately, you may work with a certified public accountant, also top in their field, on your taxes. Then, you may use the most talented, sought-after attorney to prepare your will. Next, you'll find an insurance agent who comes highly recommended to help you manage all of life's risks.

All these professionals may be the best that money can buy. Each individual decision seems perfect when made in isolation. The problem is, *none of these professionals are talking to one another*. It is very rare that your various professional advisors know each other and talk to each other, and rarer still that they collectively share their knowledge when you are making significant planning decisions. This lack of coordination may be costing you a lot of money that you have no idea you are losing. You simply don't know what you don't know, and it may be very expensive!

Almost every major decision that you make incorporates one or more professional disciplines. Take 401(k)s. Deciding to contribute to one is a tax decision. Determining how to invest the money is an investment decision. Choosing your beneficiary is an estate-planning decision.

You can have the best advice in all these areas, but you

may still have an uncoordinated financial plan, much as your living room will look haphazard after five different people decorated it according to their own tastes. Only, now you've made decisions that are much more serious than whether the modern art clashes with the traditional furniture.

SEEK A TRUE PARTNER AS YOUR FINANCIAL PLANNER

To avoid this scenario, seek an experienced, knowledgeable professional who has a defined and disciplined planning process. Their discovery process should lead to outcomes that are unique to you, based on your "hard facts" and "soft facts." Work with a fee-based fiduciary who is paid for their advice up front, rather than becoming obligated to purchase commission-based products for the financial professional to get paid.

Don't be fooled by designations like CFP®, CLU, and many others. These designations carry no regulatory standing and may be primarily purchased as marketing toward unsuspecting consumers. These designations are sold by the organizations that made up the designation. Other professionals, like attorneys and physicians, may obtain the initials JD or MD and are not required to pay for use of those initials every year. However, in the financial industry, there are more than seventy designations, and none of them have any regulatory meaning.

A comprehensive financial planner will typically have a working knowledge of many areas that may impact your family's financial well-being. For example, I know quite a bit about wills and trusts, but I'm not an attorney. I may help you plan for tax-efficient outcomes, but I am not an accountant.

The most important part of a successful financial planning relationship is the interview, in which both parties discuss expectations, compensation, objectives, and the planning process itself. The decision to proceed, or not, will be self-evident. If you proceed, being completely open and transparent with your personal documents (statements, wills, tax returns, etc.) as well as your opinions, biases, fears, and values will be critical.

Too many people fail to recognize that if you work with a competent, knowledgeable financial planner and partic- ipate in a comprehensive process, the right answers for your life situation and objectives become clear. The right decisions for your life are much less mysterious than they may have seemed when you were tackling them alone and didn't know what you didn't know.

This process can be very powerful. For some, it may be life altering. I've helped many people clarify what matters to them and simplify their life. The financial strategies are a means to your end, but first we must discover your story.

YOU CAN DO THIS!

Let's revisit how you can make the decisions that may help you get everything you want out of life.

Weed your garden. Get rid of those people in your life who would hold you back. You know who they are. If you must keep them in your life, minimize the time you spend with them and the influence they have on you. Don't let anyone step on your dreams.

Stop "shoulding" on yourself. Examine the life assembly line that you're on. Is it the one you chose? If not, you have my permission to *step off.* Not everyone should go to college, get married, or own their own home. If everyone is doing something, ask yourself what might happen if you did the opposite.

Set your ego aside. This has more to do with becoming aware of why you are making decisions than it does with judging the decisions themselves. A healthy ego is good. If you are driven by obtaining certain material possessions, then go for it. Just question the source of your motivation. Do you really want that big house or fancy car, or do you want the perception they create? Does your daughter really want to attend an Ivy League college? Make the financial decisions that are right for you, not the ones you think will help you keep up with the Joneses. For all you know, the Joneses may be in debt up to their eyeballs!

Check your biases at the door. There are no good or bad financial products or strategies; there is only what's best for you and your specific case facts. You may once have chosen incorrectly or had a bad experience with someone in the financial industry, but that's not the fault of the product or strategy. Keep an open mind, and learn all that you can going forward.

Question everything! Whoever told you that "there are no stupid questions" was correct. Bring your critical-thinking skills to every encounter with a professional advisor—financial, legal, or medical. Most importantly, ask yourself three essential questions before making any financial or life decision:

- What outcome am I seeking?
- What are my deal breakers?
- Why wouldn't I want to do this?

The last question is critical. Make the opposite case for what you are about to do. If you examine the alternatives and still feel that your decision is correct, you will proceed with confidence, and confidence increases the likelihood of a favorable outcome.

Above all else, be kind to yourself. We all make mistakes. I made a few doozies and paid for them dearly! But perhaps one of my biggest failings was in not following my own life path early enough in my life; instead, I got caught on someone else's life assembly line. If you've been there, too, don't waste another minute beating yourself up about it. Leave the gun—let the past go. You are only hurting yourself with your regrets, anger, or resentment. Take the cannoli—embrace the sweet things in life. I'm no Pollyanna, but I do know that good things happen every day if we take the time to notice them.

In the meantime, always remember that *life isn't lived on a spreadsheet*. Guard your dreams, dare to be who you know you are inside, and forgive yourself and others around you.

Thank you for taking your valuable time to read this book. If you want more information, you may contact my office by calling 866-486-4947, emailing info@poterack.net, or visiting my website at www.poterack.net.

ABOUT THE AUTHOR

RYAN POTERACK has been a financial advisor for more than twenty-five years. He had a management career at a Fortune 500 company and has started three companies of his own. He has committed his career to creating meaningful relationships with his clients, anchored by candid discussions about real-world choices we all face. Ryan and his wife, Dawn, have seven children.